18

GAME-CHANGING LESSONS

Talking Golf *with* Legends & Pros

Mark Steinbauer with **Hunki Yun**

Stewart, Tabori & Chang

NEW YORK

I DEDICATE THIS BOOK TO MY GIRLS:

Lisa, Heather, Sarah, and Rachel.

It is hard to keep this brief; so many people helped me put this book together. I have to thank Guy Yocom from *Golf Digest*, who masterminded the idea and introduced me to both Hunki Yun and Farley Chase. Guy has been a great friend and supporter for many years. I thank Hunki for all the work he invested putting my thoughts on paper, and I thank Farley who believed in this project and sold the idea to my publisher. I am thankful for Ann Stratton at Stewart, Tabori & Chang for her patience with me. Barry Ross and Glenn Gontha did a great job with the illustrations and design.

To the many main characters who fill these chapters, you have been such a blessing to me and influenced me in so many ways. A special thanks to the Penick family, my main motivation in golf. There will only be one Harvey Penick, and I am glad I got to know him.

I owe a lot to Charlie Epps, who hired me from the Academy of Golf to work for him. Like a father mentoring a son, Charlie introduced me to so many people in the world of golf, including Guy Yocom. We only worked together for a short time, but Charlie opened many doors for me. There is only one Golf Doctor, and I owe a lot to Mr. Charlie Epps.

I also would like to thank the members of Carlton Woods for allowing me to teach at such a world-class facility with arguably the finest staff anywhere in the country. And finally, a thank you to my wife, Lisa. I owe this amazing journey of mine to her and would be remiss if I didn't mention her in the list of role models I have learned from.

I n 1986 Mark Steinbauer was a new teacher at the Academy of Golf, a few miles from Austin, Texas. My father, Harvey Penick, was the Professional Emeritus at the Austin Country Club. He was eighty-two years old, and well known in Texas as a golf instructor, but still six years away from the publication of his *Little Red Book*, which gave him national recognition.

Mark had taken a few lessons from my father while he was playing on the golf team at the University of North Texas. But now that he was living nearby and a teacher himself, Mark called and asked if he could come and talk with my father about his teaching philosophy and observe his methods.

Of course, the answer was "yes" and a wonderful relationship developed between the two gentlemen. Mark recorded many of their conversations and still treasures these tapes today. The two did have a mutual respect for one another, as my father was also interested in Mark's methods. My dad always said that when he stopped learning, that's when he would stop teaching.

Guiding a student's learning was my father's ultimate goal in teaching—giving *just* enough information to bring the golfer's game to a higher level.

Dad corrected students who said they needed to "work" on their game—golf should be fun, not work. He would tell a beginner who hit a good shot that he got goose bumps on his arm—the same feeling that he had when his students Ben Crenshaw won the Masters and Tom Kite won the U.S. Open. My father did not consciously use set techniques; he just had a genuine interest in helping his students reach their highest potential.

Mark's book should convince you that his and my father's goals are the same. In 1994 Mark won the Harvey Penick Teacher of the Year award. How proud my father was—he definitely had those proverbial goose bumps.

As you travel through this text, remember that both Mark and my father would want you to "take dead aim" and "enjoy the game."

— TINSLEY PENICK

Early in my career as a golf teacher, I had a conversation with a tennis pro. We were discussing our respective jobs, and at one point, he asked me about my teaching philosophy. The question stumped me; all I had known until that point was what I was working on in my own game.

Partly because of that conversation, I set out to spend time with the best golf instructors in the world. I felt that incorporating their wisdom into my knowledge base would help me hone my own, unique teaching philosophy.

More than twenty years later, I can offer a much more definitive response, thanks to all the great minds in golf who have helped me along the way.

Ever since Old Tom Morris taught the game to his son, players and teachers have passed down their knowledge through the generations. I have been fortunate enough to watch Harvey Penick teach, play a round of golf with Jack Nicklaus, and work alongside Jim Flick.

I knew that learning from their experiences would make me a better teacher, so I tried to squeeze every bit of insight from my time with them.

In turn, I am now able to offer my knowledge to the next generation of teachers. In addition to being the director of golf of The Club at Carlton Woods in The Woodlands, Texas, I am a faculty member of The PGA of America, which means that I give teaching demonstrations and seminars to young pros. I always enjoy these sessions, especially the free exchange of ideas at the end, when I answer the young teachers' questions.

Now, I am happy to pass along to you the best of the lessons that I have learned from some of the game's greats. As you read the stories and the advice, I would encourage you to think about your own influences. Every golfer's path is different, made up of the people and experiences he or she encounters. My hope is that this book helps you on your own journey of discovery.

— MARK STEINBAUER

HARVEY PENICK

Hillbilly Learns to Putt

I grew up in a small town in northern Minnesota. Hockey was the big game, and golf was something we played only in the summer. There were no such things as junior programs, and I never had a lesson.

But somehow, my high school golf team was good enough to win the state championship. What I remember most about that event was that it was the first time I had played a course with bunkers—I had never hit a sand shot before that week. I played all the rounds trying to avoid those large holes in the earth.

By that time, I had fallen in love with golf and decided that I wanted to make a living by playing the game. But given where I was from and my lack of experience in major junior events, the best I could do was a scholarship to Bemidji State University, a Division II program near my hometown.

Fired by the ambition to play Division I golf, I made a bold decision during my freshman year. The team had driven down to Corpus Christi, Texas, for a tournament, and on the way back, I asked the golf coach to drop me off in the parking lot of a Motel 6 in Denton, the home of North Texas State University (now known as the University of North Texas).

The next morning, I walked to the campus and inquired about getting on the golf team. When I look back on what I did, I am amazed that an eighteen-year-old just decided to leave a school where he had a scholarship and move across the country to attend a university where there wasn't a guarantee that he would even make the team.

But I had done a little research, and North Texas was where I wanted to be. The university had won four consecutive national championships, from

1949 to 1952. The star of that team was Don January, who later went on to win the 1967 PGA Championship, and the coach was Fred Cobb. It was said that University of Houston golf coach Dave Williams, the most successful golf coach in NCAA history, modeled his program after the way Cobb structured his team.

After talking to a few people, I realized that I would have to sit out a year. I couldn't afford the out-of-state tuition, so I decided to work for a year to gain Texas residency. I got a job as a cart boy at the Trophy Club Country Club in Roanoke.

The Trophy Club was the only course ever designed by Ben Hogan, and he used to practice there from time to time. It was just one mile down the road from Byron Nelson's ranch. For a kid from the Iron Range of Minnesota, this was golf heaven.

Besides earning some money and being able to practice, I was able to spy on the North Texas golf team, which played qualifying rounds there to decide which players would get to play in the next tournament. So I had an idea of how much I needed to improve to make that team.

I decided that what I really needed was to be a better putter. The Trophy Club's assistant pro, who had hired me, told me to go see Harvey Penick in Austin. I had never heard of him, but I called Austin Country Club right away and scheduled a lesson.

When the day came to make the four-hour drive to Austin, I couldn't have been more excited. I had never taken a lesson in my life, so I had no idea how much it cost or what the protocol was. I brought cash, my checkbook, and my mother's credit card.

I was a little early for the lesson, so I started stroking some putts on the practice green. As I waited, my nervousness grew because it became apparent to me that Harvey was a big deal, and I didn't want to do anything foolish in front of him. Harvey came out right on time and introduced himself. He immediately put me at ease, asking me questions about where I was from, how long I had been playing, my goals.

He then noticed my putter, a Wilson 8802, and asked how I had gotten to using it. I answered that my idol was Ben Crenshaw, not knowing at the time that Harvey had been Ben's longtime teacher. I told him that I wanted to copy both his equipment and his stroke, which meant that I stood upright with my arms hanging down.

After I answered, Harvey asked me whether I knew the man behind me. I turned around and there was Crenshaw himself, waiting to talk to his teacher!

Crenshaw was standing off to the edge of the green because he was wearing cowboy boots. He introduced himself as if he were just any other member at the club welcoming a guest, and we got to talking about putting. Crenshaw asked to see my putter and set several balls on the fringe, about ten feet from the nearest hole.

He stroked the first putt with the smoothest, purest stroke I had ever seen. The putt had a little break and it was tracking directly at the hole, only to hit the lip and roll out. He then hit three more putts, each one in the dead center of the hole.

"This putter is a little more upright than mine," Crenshaw said. "It has a good feel, though."

I was beaming, and I'm sure my smile could be seen back in Minnesota.

Ben gave the putter back to me and returned to the clubhouse, leaving me to my lesson. I remember Harvey telling me that although Crenshaw's method may have been popular at the time, there were other great putters and other ways of putting.

He then asked me how I had putted when I was younger.

"I bent way over and used my hands for feel," I replied.

"Did you putt better then than you do now?"

"Yes," I said reluctantly.

Harvey was trying to tell me that my natural technique was better than copying somebody else's. Crenshaw's style worked for him because that was his own technique, one developed over time. He hadn't copied the methods used by Jack Nicklaus or Arnold Palmer.

Harvey wanted me to develop my natural style, but he had three fundamentals that he didn't want me to skip: put my thumbs on top of the grip, keep my eyes over the ball, and try to hit the ball in the middle of the putter face.

Of the three, he was most adamant about the grip, because the hands are the only part of the body in contact with the club and therefore have the most control over what the club does during the shot.

My eyes were in the correct position and I was making solid contact, but my thumbs weren't on top of the club, so Harvey had me adjust my grip. Of course, I then started putting a lot better and began to regain confidence in my game. Over the next seventeen years, Harvey would continue to remind me now and again to keep my thumbs on top.

When I returned to Denton, everybody wanted to know what Harvey had told me. When I explained that he had fixed my grip, they all seemed disappointed because the advice was so simple. Like nearly everybody who had gone to see Harvey, they were probably thinking that he would have some more complicated knowledge to impart.

After the lesson, which lasted about an hour, Harvey invited me to go to the range and practice. Excited about what had just happened, I wound up hitting three bags of balls. If I'd had any doubts about leaving Minnesota to pursue my dreams, those moments on the range, awash in memories of the previous hour, obliterated them. Not only had I received my first lesson from one of the best teachers ever, I had met my idol!

After my practice session, I headed to the pro shop to settle up with Harvey. Crenshaw was talking to a group of members outside the entrance. I was too timid to walk up to the group, but Ben saw me and left his conversation to say good-bye to me. He even remembered my name and wished me luck in my quest to make the team at North Texas State. He also told me to listen to what Harvey said.

Nothing could bring me down from that high. As I entered the pro shop, however, I was a bit apprehensive about how much my amazing day was going to cost. Clutching all my various methods of payment, I sought out Harvey. When I asked how much I owed him, Harvey told me three dollars.

I was sure I had misheard, so I asked again.

"Three dollars for the three bags you hit," he said. "And be sure to come back next month. We have a couple of things to work on."

Needless to say, Harvey made a tremendous impression on me that day. He knew I didn't have much money, and he went out of his way to help a young hillbilly getting his start in the golf world. I appreciated what he had done, and I couldn't wait to come back in a few weeks.

Of all the lessons I learned that day, the biggest had nothing to do with golf. It was trust. At the next lesson, Harvey could have told me to putt while standing on my head, and I would have done it. I gave myself completely to him, and he came to know my game as well as I did—probably better. I always played a stronger game after seeing him, and I learned something about golf and life every time I talked to him.

Although I didn't know it at the time, that day was the start of our lasting relationship, first as teacher and pupil then as mentor and apprentice, which lasted until he passed away in 1995.

In the following chapters, I will outline the most important lessons I have learned from him, and from various other people in golf. But I wouldn't have learned any of them without the lesson of trust that I received during my first meeting with Harvey more than twenty years ago.

MARK'S LESSONS

It's a natural tendency to want to emulate your favorite player. But what Harvey wanted to instill in me from our first lesson was the importance of playing with your own style, one that comes easily to you. Because it is natural, you can trust it, instead of having to think all the time about whether you are in the right position. That's no way to play golf.

At our first lesson, Harvey made me realize that when I was trying to putt like Ben Crenshaw, I was thinking about whether I was standing in the correct posture and how far I should take back the putter, instead of thinking about pace and line.

With my natural, bent-over setup, I didn't have to think about mechanics. Instead, I trusted my stroke, which allowed me to focus on making the putt. Trust is a big part of playing golf, and you have to find a way to incorporate it into your game.

HIGH HANDICAPPER

Having my thumbs on top of the grip while putting ensures that my hands face each other in a neutral position. In other words, it keeps the putter face square.

If your face isn't square, it really doesn't matter what else you do during the putting stroke, because your putts will never go where you want them to roll.

Harvey had two other must-follow fundamentals. Fixing your eyes over the ball ensures that the putter follows a straight path through impact. If the eyes are inside the ball (closer to your feet), the tendency is for the path to be from inside the target line, causing putts to roll right. If the eyes are outside the ball, the putter will approach the ball from outside the target line, causing pulled putts.

Hitting the ball in the middle of the putter face, which is where the sweet spot is located, ensures that the ball reaches the hole. Contact toward the heel or toe will come up well short of the hole.

MID HANDICAPPER

There is a lot to consider on every putt: Is my putter face square? Are my eyes over the ball? Is my ball position correct? How much break is there? Is the putt downhill? How hard should I hit it? Is this putt two balls outside left or just one?

There are a lot of opportunities for doubt to creep into your mind. And doubt is the worst thing you can have when you're over a putt.

If you trust your stroke, all you need to do is determine the line and the speed. Then, you must commit to that putt completely, trusting that it will get the ball to the hole.

Even if your determination of the break is off-line by a little bit, you're much better off trusting that line and your stroke than reading the break perfectly and second-guessing everything afterward. A trusting stroke is a confident stroke, and you'll make many more putts if you putt with confidence.

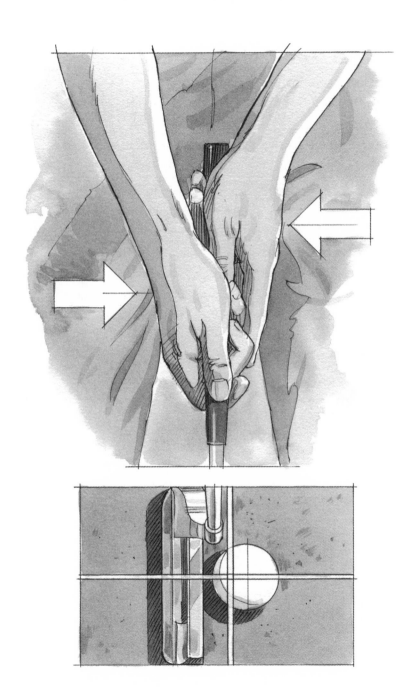

LOW HANDICAPPER

Many low handicappers get caught up in how their swings look. Is my elbow in the correct position? Is my finish too high? Golfers often compare their actions with those of tour players.

Harvey believed that every player had a swing that worked for him or her, and he didn't want his students copying others. As a result, he never let his two star pupils, Ben Crenshaw and Tom Kite, watch each other's lessons. He didn't want either of them picking up something that was only meant for the other.

It doesn't matter what your swing looks like. All that matters is getting the ball in the hole. If beauty were important, a lot of great players would never have made it to the PGA Tour. Lee Trevino, Ray Floyd, Fred Couples, and Jim Furyk have swings that are far from textbook-perfect, but they have made their quirks work for them.

Instead of looking to others for your model, look inside yourself—know your strengths and your tendencies, and trust that they will get the job done.

ED IBARGUEN

There are many aspects of being a golf teacher: knowledge of the swing, connecting with students, physical demands. One little-known quality is enthusiasm, which allows teachers to motivate students to learn a very difficult, often discouraging game.

Ed Ibarguen encourages students and gets them excited about golf better than any other teacher I have witnessed. We have taught many PGA of America classes together, and during one session in a conference room, Ed became so involved in the lesson that he actually jumped on the table to demonstrate a point.

Ed's energy is infectious, and the lesson is that if you are looking to improve your golf game, you'll progress faster if you find a teacher or a group of playing partners who keep you motivated.

HARVEY PENICK

"It Depends"

Every student comes into a lesson looking for definitive solutions to his or her problems. And I wish I had concrete responses. But the golf swing is complicated, and there are countless ways of approaching it.

Of course, the man who taught me that was Harvey Penick. I can't tell you how many times I heard him say, "It depends."

During lessons, students peppering him with questions and expecting definite responses would often hear the same answer.

Should my grip be stronger?

"It depends."

Where should the ball position be for a driver?

"It depends."

How long should my backswing be?

"It depends."

Every once in a while, I would come to Harvey with what I thought was an absolute in golf. I remember talking to him about players with closed clubfaces at the top of their backswings. I was trying to make the point that these players couldn't be consistent because of the timing it required to square the clubface and keep from hooking the ball.

In response, Harvey cited several famous golfers who had closed clubfaces at the top. We were watching the 1989 U.S. Women's Open at the time, and at the end of his recitation, he simply pointed to the television, on which Betsy King was winning the event—with a closed clubface. That clubface, in fact, did not keep King from winning thirty-four tournaments in total, including six majors.

Teaching pros are passionate about their jobs and often talk to one another, both formally and informally, about the best way to help their students improve. Butch Harmon learned plenty from his father, noted teacher and player Claude Harmon. A young Hank Haney was influenced by Jim Hardy. And a generation of teachers have benefited from dinner conversations with men like Jim Flick, David Leadbetter, and Bob Toski. I myself have given dozens of presentations to colleagues, and I always open with the same two words: "It depends."

I first became a convert of "it depends" during a conversation Harvey and I had about putting. I had studied the strokes of some of the best putters in the game, including Ben Crenshaw. I had become convinced that Ben's stroke, using a firm left wrist, was the best way to putt and had come to see this action as a quality shared by the best putters in the game.

Well, did Harvey ever burst that bubble. He listed a bunch of great putters who putted differently, starting with Horton Smith, the winner of the first Masters, in 1934. He also mentioned Bobby Locke and Billy Casper, who both popped putts with considerable wrist action.

Had he not been so modest, Harvey easily could have included himself on the list, because he was a great putter. The most remarkable part of this lecture was that Harvey had seen all these legenday golfers play in person; he was not relying on photos or television to make his observations.

After several similar conversations, I realized that I had come to Harvey, my mentor, with the notion that he would make my job easier by giving me a one-size-fits-all method of teaching. Of course, he didn't.

Talking to Harvey was often like talking to Yoda, the Jedi master from the *Star Wars* movies. Harvey's cryptic comments made little sense at first, but they started his student on the road to learning the answer for him- or herself, a process that did a lot more good than being spoon-fed the answer.

Especially in this age of information overload, we are looking for instant fixes and definitive statements that cut through the clutter and leave little room for ambiguity: "Cure your slice." "Ten more yards." "Solid contact." But the problem with that approach to the golf swing is that dissecting the swing is actually all about shades of meaning. And what Harvey understood better than anyone was that a piece of advice that would cure one student's slice might promote somebody else's.

Go to a typical golf school, and what you'll find is a bunch of students on the driving range, all performing the same drills. Spot one of those students playing anywhere and you know what school they attended. It would be impossible, however, to identify a pupil of Harvey's at the range, because he never prescribed the same fix twice.

Harvey once gave lessons to two girls who seemingly had the same fault: a swing plane that was too upright. With one girl, he put a tee in the ground and told her to clip it out of the turf. This changed the bottom of her arc, which in turn required her to change her plane to return the club to the ball properly. It worked; she hit straighter shots right away. For the other girl, Harvey changed her grip. It was a completely different fix, but the result was the same: improved swing plane.

I learned later that Harvey had also talked to the girls briefly to get an understanding of the way each of them thought and approached the swing. Based on their answers, he determined that one would respond better to a swing-based fix, while the other needed a grip change. Same ailment, different medicine. It depends.

There have been plenty of fads in golf instruction over the years, from "Square to Square" to "Stack and Tilt." But these methods come and go because the truth is that absolutes do not get results.

There have been many successful players over the years who had individual techniques that didn't conform to the orthodoxy. Jack Nicklaus has a flying right elbow. Nancy Lopez takes the club extremely to the inside in the backswing. Lee Trevino has an extreme re-route move in the downswing. Seve Ballesteros picks up the club abruptly in the backswing. Paul Azinger has an extremely strong grip.

If some instructor had gotten Lee Trevino to stop taking the club back to the outside in the backswing, there is a good chance we never would have heard of him. Taken individually and out of context, the quirks exhibited by these major players would all be considered no-nos, and many teachers subscribing to absolute theories would try to correct them.

Many of you have been fitted for golf clubs with the help of a launch monitor, which spits out detailed information about your shots. This testing is based on the notion that there is a customized combination of clubhead and shaft that will give you the best results. We have learned, in other words, that no single standard for equipment exists, and I believe that we should approach golf instruction the same way. Trying to learn golf from an absolute method is like walking into a store and buying the first driver you see. It might seem easier, but you won't play your best golf.

So the next time you are asking questions about your swing, be wary of any answer that doesn't begin with "It depends."

MARK'S LESSONS

There are exceptions to every accepted norm. Since "it depends" and there are no absolutes in golf, give the following unorthodox moves a try.

HIGH HANDICAPPER

In a neutral grip, the left hand (for right-handers) is placed on the grip so the V formed by the gap between the thumb and palm points between the chin and the right ear and two knuckles are visible. This has been the accepted way to hold the club for decades.

But for beginners, it may be best to adopt a stronger grip, in which the V points to the right shoulder and three knuckles are visible. The prevailing wisdom is that a strong grip promotes a hook and makes it harder to hit high shots. But it just might help a lot of golfers.

First, most amateurs hit slices, which means that they have a hard time squaring the clubface through impact. A stronger grip promotes an aggressive closing of the face through the ball. You will be able to hit the ball more solidly and may even get rid of your slice.

Second, today's clubs are engineered with more weight near the bottom of the clubhead, which makes it easier to get the ball into the air. Given this new equipment, a stronger grip isn't a detriment. It actually may be a plus, because a hooded face will help prevent the ballooning ball flight that robs distance.

So if you're looking for more distance and have trouble hitting the ball to the left, give the stronger grip a try.

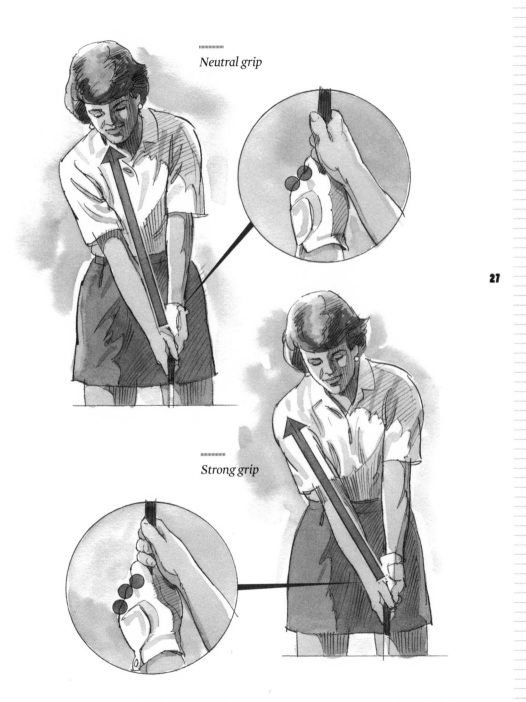

Neutral grip

Strong grip

HARVEY PENICK: "IT DEPENDS"

MID HANDICAPPER

Today's equipment also influences my second piece of advice that bucks convention. While it is ideal to swing the club on the proper plane, it may be beneficial to try a swing that is flat, or under that plane.

Tour pros want to swing on plane because it allows them to square the club naturally at the very high speeds at which they swing. You've probably heard Tiger Woods talking about getting "stuck" in the downswing. That means the club was in the plane and behind him, so the head approached the ball from inside the target line. At Woods's 125-mile-per-hour clubhead speed, that requires perfect timing, so he considers that a fault.

Since you swing at a slower speed, probably around ninety miles per hour, swinging flatter and more around your body isn't necessarily bad. It will help prevent coming over the top and hitting slices.

A flatter swing is also more compatible with today's drivers, which are longer than those from a generation ago—another excellent reason some golfers should forget about swinging on plane.

LOW HANDICAPPER

Conventional short-game instruction tells you that it is best to chip with different clubs. That way, you use just one motion and change club selection based on how much fringe and green you have to go over. In other words, you can chip with anything from a six-iron to a sand wedge.

While that can work, I have a better solution: Putt whenever possible. Since it is the easiest shot to pull off, putting allows you to miss slightly and still execute a good shot, especially on tight lies, from where it is easy to hit fat or thin chips. When you putt, the worst score you'll make is bogey, and you'll get it up and down more often than not. In the long run, it is the most consistent club around the green.

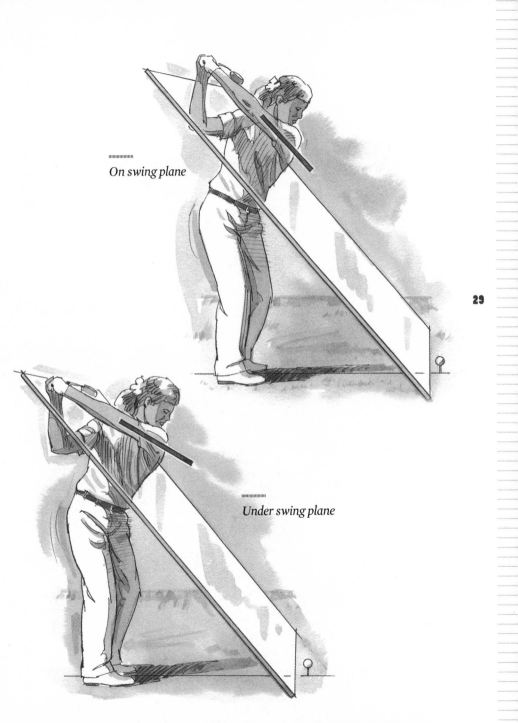

On swing plane

Under swing plane

BEN HOGAN

The Perfectionist

Before I met Harvey Penick, I was exposed to another Texas golf legend—Ben Hogan. By then, Hogan had retired from competition, although he was still in the business as the owner of an equipment company bearing his name. He also had helped build the Trophy Club Country Club in Roanoke.

The club's course was the only one designed by Hogan, who was known for his focus during the game and his work ethic while he practiced. He liked being in control and played with a precision that no player since has matched.

As I soon learned, he brought that same sense of meticulousness and discipline to the Trophy Club. Upon my arrival there, the first thing I noticed about the club was how well maintained the entire place was, from the course to the clubhouse and even to the parking lot. Hogan obviously had high standards for his club, and I later learned that there was no inspection quite as rigorous as a Hogan inspection.

Truth be told, the atmosphere was a bit stiff. Hogan took his golf very seriously, and everyone at the club—members and staff—knew his or her place and was expected to live up to Hogan's expectations.

There was a clear distinction between the inside and outside staff. As a bag room employee, I was not allowed in the golf shop, even though the bag room and the pro shop were next to each other. To further emphasize the divide, the carpets in the shop and the bag room were different colors. I specifically remember leaning over the golf shop carpet so I wouldn't touch it whenever I passed a note to a shop staffer.

Hogan was equally as fastidious about his course, which is routed over rolling land and through majestic oak trees and remains one of my favorites to this day. Player-architects tend to design courses that fit their games. Jack Nicklaus, for example, built many courses early in his architectural career that favored shots that were shaped left to right, which was his prominent, preferred shot shape at the time.

When playing Nicklaus's early courses, it helps to hit long, high shots that land softly. The problem is, there aren't too many players, even pros, who can hit the ball as long or as soft as the Golden Bear. Nicklaus has since varied his designs to fit all kinds of games.

Perhaps the best all-around ball-striker in the history of golf, Hogan built his course without any such biases. There are an equal number of holes that dogleg left and right. Many are strategic, however, and require a precision not unlike Hogan's in properly shaping tee shots to set up the best approach to the greens.

After a few days at the club, I came to realize that Hogan gave special care to two areas: the greens and the practice tee. He didn't care about the greens from a putting perspective—in fact, it was the part of the game with which he had had the most trouble during his career. He fussed over the greens because he wanted them to reward only shots struck solidly and with just the right amount of spin on the ball. In short, he wanted them to receive the kind of shots only he could hit on a regular basis.

I got to know Jim Brown, who used to shag balls for Hogan. Jim would tell stories about how precise Hogan's practice sessions used to be. When Mr. Hogan practiced, he would hit balls so they would make little piles at regular intervals. Jim barely had to move to pick up Hogan's practice balls.

I would try to make piles of balls during my practice sessions, but I would find that although I could make the shot land at a certain spot, the ball would bounce off erratically because I couldn't control its spin.

Hogan believed that being able to control that spin should pay off, and that's why he kept tweaking the Trophy Club course, like the day he went out to test one of the greens that had a pond in front of it. Hogan hit several shots over the water and waited for each one to spin back into the pond. When none did, he ordered that the be grass stripped off the green and added a wheelbarrow of dirt to change the pitch. Hogan then smoothed the area with his foot and replaced the sod.

Hogan also spent a lot of time at his other favorite place: the practice ground. Nobody hit more balls than he did, and he had a special tee on the range built just for him. There were trees planted around it for privacy, and he could be found hitting balls there at the same time every afternoon.

He had made sure that his tee faced south to ensure that he would be hitting into the wind 80 percent of the time during the year. He liked to practice into the wind, which magnified the ball flight. Hogan never hit balls when the wind was coming from the left, which he felt would groove an improper swing path.

Also, Hogan's tee was in the corner and angled so he could hit uphill and see where the balls would land. He and Jim had a routine. After hitting a pile of balls at Jim's feet, Hogan would then aim about ten yards to the right and start piling up balls at the new spot, which would be Jim's cue to switch spots.

Once, Jim tried to catch Hogan's shots in the air, but the balls had so much backspin on them that they would hit Jim's hands and squirt free like fish. Although he was a small man, Hogan had strong hands and arms that moved the club through impact as powerfully as anyone in the game. The strength and quickness of his hands were apparent in the way he dealt cards: He would have made a casino dealer jealous.

Hogan built that strength and quickness through hitting millions of balls in his lifetime. One of my jobs was to take care of the practice ground, and what I liked most was examining Hogan's tee box after he had finished. Every divot looked like the outline of a shrimp: thin and curved slightly to the left, indicating they started just after impact. Harvey Penick, who studied divots closely, would have approved.

Hogan very much wanted the Trophy Club to host the U.S. Open, an event that he had won four times. The United States Golf Association (USGA) informed Hogan that although the course was good, the logistics of the surrounding area weren't: There weren't enough hotel rooms, and access to the course wasn't adequate.

When he got that news, Hogan lost interest in the Trophy Club and began to spend more time at Fort Worth's Shady Oaks Country Club, where he was a member. Shady Oaks was more convenient for him anyway because he lived in Fort Worth.

There, Hogan continued to live by a precision that would have made a Swiss watchmaker envious. He drove to his office at the same time every day, parked his car in the same spot, went to Shady Oaks for lunch at the same time, occupied the same table overlooking the eighteenth green, then went out to hit balls on a secluded spot at Shady Oaks' nine-hole, par-three course.

Although Hogan no doubt felt quite at home at Shady Oaks, he remained reticent. In fact, his aloofness was legendary, bordering on rudeness. In one infamous anecdote, Hogan was paired with Claude Harmon at the 1947 Masters. They came to the twelfth hole, the short but tricky par-three. Because of the small target and constantly swirling winds, just hitting the tee shot on the green was cause for celebration.

Harmon was a great teaching pro, working for a long time at Winged Foot Golf Club outside New York City. He played in a lot of events and had earned the respect of tour pros. He was no interloper and knew many of the players well, including Hogan.

On this day he was paired with Hogan, and Harmon hit a beautiful shot that found the bottom of the cup for a hole-in-one. It was a rare feat, considering that in the seventy-five-year history of the Masters, there have been only three aces on the twelfth hole.

While those around were congratulating Harmon, Hogan didn't say a word. He focused on his pre-shot routine and hit a good shot, ten feet from the hole. The pair walked up to the green, and Harmon picked his ball out of the hole to much fanfare. Still, Hogan hadn't said anything, focusing instead on lining up his birdie putt. He made the putt, and as they were walking to the thirteenth tee, he finally spoke.

Instead of congratulating Harmon for his unique feat, Hogan simply said: "You know, Claude, I think that's the first time I've made a two on that hole."

While Hogan's intensity may have brought a laugh to Harmon as he was retelling the story, it was very intimidating to a kid like me. Part of my job at the Trophy Club involved running clubs between the club and Hogan's factory in Forth Worth. The entrance to the factory was located on a side street, and there was only one parking spot: Hogan's. It wasn't marked, but everyone knew not to park there. If somebody did happen to make that mistake and Hogan found out, he wouldn't say a word to the offender. He would just give him the stare. And it would never happen again.

Whenever I was around him, I knew not to speak and not to make eye contact. Hogan was the most intimidating man I have ever met. And I didn't care if I had to park a mile away and walk—there was no way I was going to park in his spot.

A few months after Hogan lost interest in the Trophy Club, I received a copy of his famous book, *Ben Hogan's Five Lessons: The Modern Fundamentals of Golf*, as a present. I wanted him to sign it, but I couldn't summon the courage to ask. After a few days, I asked Jim to help me, which actually meant I wanted him to handle it for me. He did. Jim walked into Hogan's office and explained the situation—and Hogan couldn't have been nicer. He signed my book, handed it back to Jim, and wished me luck.

I was surprised by how cordial Hogan had been, but I learned that he did let his stern facade slip at times. Despite working with Hogan for four years, Jim exchanged very few words with his boss during their relationship. Hogan was not talkative, especially while hitting balls. But what shone through was the fact that, although he could make golf seem like work, he loved the game.

One time, that enthusiasm came to the forefront when Jim least expected it. That day, Jim was playing at Shady Oaks while Hogan watched him from his usual perch overlooking the eighteenth hole, as he had done countless times before. After the round, Jim ran into him in the restroom; and much to Jim's disbelief, Hogan gave him a lesson right there. Apparently, he'd seen something in Jim's swing that he couldn't wait to tell him about. So in the men's room, Jim listened as Hogan dissected in detail how he needed to move his right knee toward the target through impact instead of spinning out.

At that moment, Jim understood the depth of passion that Hogan brought to the game and to a place like the Trophy Club. Although I never got to spend a lot of time with Hogan, working at the Trophy Club allowed me to better understand one of the greatest champions in golf history.

MARK'S LESSONS

In the long history of golf, nobody worked harder than Ben Hogan. But the key to his practice sessions wasn't their duration; it was the intensity and focus that he brought to them. He was always working on something.

A lot of amateurs practice without any aim in mind. They're just out there hitting balls, without consciously "practicing" a specific technique. They might hit a few wedges and short irons before pulling out the driver and pounding away. For the most effective practice, you need to be focused—maybe not quite to the extent that Hogan was, but his intensity should be a model for every golfer to at least aim for. Here are some ways to do that.

HIGH HANDICAPPER

Just as you have a desk at your job, you should set up a workstation on the range, consisting of a tee and extra clubs, to create an environment that offers you the best chance for success. For each shot, set the club on the ground for alignment to a target on the range, because poor aim is one of the biggest culprits when it comes to off-line shots. How many times have you made a seemingly good swing, only to have the ball land more than ten yards to the right or left of your target? Chances are, you were aiming left or right to begin with.

Practicing is about building confidence, and you can't do that if you're not hitting the ball solidly during your sessions. It can be frustrating to hit a series of fat or thin shots. It may take a little more time, but be sure to hit every shot off a tee—even the short irons. This will greatly increase your chances of finding the sweet spot of the club, and the positive feedback that you receive from hitting good shots will make your practice more effective.

Hitting off a tee is especially useful at many busy grass ranges, where it is difficult to find a patch of well-tended grass. A tee will give you a perfect lie every time. If you normally practice off a mat, buy a short rubber tee so you have control of your environment, instead of relying on whatever length tee is available at the facility.

39

MID HANDICAPPER

I know it's fun to pull out the driver at the range and swing for the fences. But if you're working on fixing a part of your swing, you should leave that club in the bag and reach for a mid or short iron.

Because of its length, the driver tends to exaggerate every portion of the swing, which not only makes it difficult to feel a change but also prevents you from building consistent rhythm because the tendency is to swing harder. Not only that, the driver is harder to hit, so you probably won't be hitting the shots you want, which increases your chances of abandoning the change because of all the negative feedback you're getting.

When tour pros are trying to make an adjustment, they usually do so with a seven- or eight-iron. And when you're working on mechanics, I suggest hitting balls off a tee, especially if you're doing a drill.

LOW HANDICAPPER

Good players have grooved a reasonably reliable swing, especially by the end of a practice session. Usually, their biggest problem is taking this swing from the range to the course.

Rhythm is often the problem. On the range, you are hitting several shots in a row with the same club, enabling you to make adjustments between swings. Although your basic swing is the same, because of the varied shaft lengths and clubface lofts, every club sets up slightly differently.

But on the course, you may be switching between extremes in clubs from shot to shot—driver followed by a nine-iron—without the cushion of being able to make adjustments between swings, which leaves you unable to find a rhythm with each club.

A good way to practice this club-to-club dilemma is to play simulated "rounds" on the range. Pretend you are playing all eighteen holes of your home course. For example, if the first hole is a four-hundred-yard par-four, hit a driver—aiming between two flags to represent the edges of the fairway—followed by whichever club you normally use for the approach. Then "play" the rest of the course, using the clubs that you normally would use.

HARVEY PENICK
Simplicity Is Best

Millions of golfers have read *Harvey Penick's Little Red Book* and its sequels, which are the best-selling golf books of all time. I think Harvey's books are so popular because the lessons they contain are simple yet effective. Advice doesn't get any more direct—or more instructive—than "take dead aim."

But behind these memorably straightforward aphorisms lie years of observation, thought, and experimentation. I was one of the few people fortunate enough to have read the original "Little Red Book," the legendary notebook in which Harvey jotted down his ideas about the game. He always wrote in pencil, and there were a lot of eraser marks, as he refined the precision of exactly what he wanted to say.

Harvey was not unlike most of you who have tried various tips, images, and swing thoughts in your quest for improvement. First and foremost, he was a student of golf, and he realized that there was always something else he could learn, no matter how much he already knew about the game. Even after watching golfers for decades, he still enjoyed watching tournaments to see if he could pick up even the smallest nugget of information that would help him in his teaching. Some of my favorite memories of Harvey took place not on the lesson tee but in his living room, watching golf on television and casually discussing the game that had brought us together.

Harvey was quite aware of the evolution of the golf swing as he got older. For much of his career, the prevailing school of thought was that the small muscles—hands and arms—controlled the swing. But as he watched more players on television swinging with their bodies, Harvey updated that theory.

"Look at this guy," he would say. "Look at the back muscles at work."

For Harvey, of course, there was always no one method, no single way to swing the club. Probably nobody knew more about golf than Harvey did, but what really made him a genius was not how much he knew, but how he could apply that knowledge to help each individual golfer in a totally idiosyncratic way.

A lot of teachers can make a diagnosis that the reason a student is struggling with the hooks is because his clubface is closed at the top of his swing. But not many can help him straighten out his drives by prescribing a cure that will not only correct the fault, but also resonate specifically with that student.

For example, if the student were an analytical player like Tom Kite, Harvey probably would have said something like, "Tom, you need to make sure the angle of your clubface matches your left forearm at the top of the backswing so that it is square. Then, you need to initiate your downswing from the bottom up so your weight shifts aggressively and your lower body clears the way, enabling the clubface to release naturally so it is square at impact."

And Tom would have processed the information, made the necessary adjustments, and straightened out his drives.

I once watched a video of Harvey giving a lesson to his other famous pupil, Ben Crenshaw, who was having the exact same problem: hooked drives. It was the day before Ben was due to leave for a tournament, and he was clearly frustrated about his inability to hit the fairway. Instead of talking about Ben's clubface, grip, or body positions, Harvey simply asked him to accompany him to the left side of the driving range.

Harvey had been Ben's teacher for years. They had a unique bond, and it was a privilege just to watch them interact—to receive a glimpse into one of the most successful student-teacher relationships in golf. I would feel the same way when Harvey and I would be talking golf, and he would say, "Don't tell anyone, but . . ."

The range at Austin Country Club sits to the right of the tenth hole, so a hook from the left end of the range very well could end up in that fairway. Harvey simply told Ben to keep the ball out of the fairway—nothing about club or body positions. As the lesson progressed, I watched in awe as Ben's clubface position at the top of the backswing gradually became square, his lower body moved aggressively through the ball, and his drives flew high and straight. By the end of the lesson, I was stunned that a simple directive like "Keep the ball out of the tenth fairway" could correct Ben's technical faults.

At the time, I asked Harvey how he knew just how to fix Crenshaw's hook. Instead of answering, Harvey replied with a story about how he had helped Crenshaw before a big tournament in college. I asked again, but still didn't get the response I was looking for. But that was common with Harvey. One of the frustrating aspects of my conversations with him was the way he wouldn't give me a definitive response to my questions.

Although it was frustrating at the time, I came to realize that it was much more satisfying to earn an answer than to have him spoon-feed it to me. Additionally, self-discovery made the knowledge much more useful to me as a teacher since I understood the concepts more deeply and could use that in my lessons. If I were just parroting what Harvey had told me, I don't think I would have been as helpful.

The information he was trying to convey about Crenshaw was that he had come to know Ben's game well, and that I would be able to help my students better once I got to know them and connected with them in an individual way.

I watched another lesson with a longtime member who thought Harvey had hung the moon. He was having the worst time with the shanks and came to Harvey desperate for a cure.

After the member explained his problem and hit a few shots—shanks, predictably—Harvey got out of his cart and placed his cane just outside the ball, making a show of leaning on it for support. He then told the member to hit the ball without hitting the cane. I never saw as much fear in a golfer's eyes as I witnessed in this member's. The last thing he wanted to do was to hit the cane and send his friend and teacher to the ground—and Harvey knew it!

Reluctantly, the member stepped up and made a swing, missing the cane and hitting the ball solidly. He did it again and again and never came close to hitting the cane. Harvey had cured his shanks because he knew how best to communicate with his student. And every time this member would be afflicted with the shanks after that, all he had to do was picture Harvey and his cane, an image that helped immensely.

But keeping the game simple wasn't as easy as Harvey made it seem. As I climbed the ladder of the teaching profession, the skill level of my students went up, as did my rates. To impress my pupils and justify the expense, I felt like I had to dazzle them with my knowledge of the swing. I was under the misconception that I was being paid by the word.

Every instructor wants to be tour guru. Before a lesson with my college roommate Joel Edwards, who was swinging the club from too far inside the target line and hooking the ball, I wasn't quite sure how to fix his swing path; so I took some photos of Joel's swing and showed them to Harvey.

He looked at them and simply told me to have him "clip the tee." Immediately, I thought about how foolish I would sound giving this type of basic advice to a really skilled player. This was the kind of rudimentary tip I normally give to beginners and mid handicappers to help them make contact with the ball more consistently. It was like telling a major-league baseball player to "make a level swing."

So I explained to Harvey that Joel was a tour player and not a beginner. Harvey's response was that this simple directive would help the player swing more along the target line and not so much from the inside.

As it turned out, Joel was fine with the simple response. He worked on clipping the tee, and his ball flight improved almost immediately.

Through this experience and others, I learned from Harvey that understanding the golf swing is not enough to be an effective instructor. Ultimately, the most important goal of a lesson is to help the student. And Harvey understood that sometimes the best lessons only require a few words.

Once, a student flew all the way from France to see the famous Harvey Penick, only to get a lesson that consisted of little more than "move the ball back." If the swing took just a few words to fix, what did it matter whether the student had come from across town or around the world? Harvey knew that the only thing that mattered was that the student left with a better golf game.

MARK'S LESSONS

I wouldn't be a golf teacher if it weren't for Harvey. He was my instructor, mentor, confidant, and friend. I learned from him so much about life.

Of course, golf was our bond, and he taught me a lot about the game. More important, he showed me the best way to teach it to others. Here are some of the lessons I learned from him that you could apply to your own game and the way you communicate with your own instructor.

HIGH HANDICAPPER

Simplicity is best. The best tips are often explained in just a few words. Some of Harvey's most memorable are: "Take dead aim" and "Clip the tee." It is too easy for beginners and high handicappers to get confused by a deluge of information about what the body and club should be doing during the swing. I'll be the first to admit that golf is a complicated, difficult game. However, there's no reason to make learning to play it confusing. Try to keep your thoughts and your tips simple the way Harvey did.

MID HANDICAPPER

One of the main reasons Harvey was such a good teacher was that he told students what to do rather than what they were doing wrong. He filled me with such confidence during our lessons that I always played better afterward. My mind was clear and focused instead of being cluttered by negative, harmful baggage.

As players improve, they will hit a wide range of shots, from very good, pro-quality irons to embarrassing misses such as topped drives. After a poor shot, it is easy to allow negative thoughts to multiply, which in turn leads to a downward spiral of more bad shots.

Instead, think about what you did correctly. It could be as basic as the grip. As long as you keep doing things right, you'll improve in the long run.

LOW HANDICAPPER

While you may know a lot about golf and the swing, it is easy to fall into the trap of being inundated by too much information. Keep in mind that although the swing is complicated, you don't need to treat it that way—especially when you're playing.

If you're having a problem, don't break down your swing and examine each part the way a mechanic would fix a car. Take a cue from the lesson Harvey gave Ben Crenshaw to cure his hook. It was brilliant in its simplicity and effectiveness.

But even if you're analytical like Tom Kite, be sure to keep the mechanics on the range. Kite may work on his swing on the practice range, but once he's on the course, he has left the analysis behind and plays with a free and clear mind.

50

TOM KITE

Of all the players I have watched over the past forty years, I believe no player's swing has changed more than Tom Kite's. At the tour level, even a slight tweak can feel like a huge change. An overhaul requires tremendous practice, and Kite, one of the hardest workers in golf, hit thousands of balls and spent thousands of hours honing his new swing so that he could rely on it under pressure.

Yet most amateurs try on new swings as if they were shirts, and expect them to work immediately. When it doesn't, they try something else.

So take a lesson from Kite by following his example. Unless you can work on your swing full time and are as devoted to practice as Kite was, you're better off honing your natural swing and making it as consistent as possible.

BILL ESCHENBRENNER

The Importance of Impact

Texans have played a huge role in golf history. In addition to producing three of the greatest players ever—Ben Hogan, Byron Nelson, Kathy Whitworth—the Lone Star State has been home to these major championship winners: Jimmy Demaret, Ralph Guldahl, Ben Crenshaw, Tom Kite, Jack Burke Jr., Charles Coody, Lloyd Mangrum, Justin Leonard, Mark Brooks, Lee Trevino, and Rich Beem.

Among the great female players from Texas are Babe Zaharias, Betsy Rawls, Sandra Haynie, Betty Jameson, and Sandra Palmer—all multiple major winners.

On the instruction side, some of the great teachers who have made Texas home include Hank Haney, Chuck Cook, and Dick Harmon, as well as Harvey Penick. And finally, Dan Jenkins, the well-known golf writer, is from Fort Worth.

Of all the golf geniuses from Texas, perhaps one of the least heralded is my friend Bill Eschenbrenner. The longtime pro at El Paso Country Club, "Esch" is one of the elder statesmen of Texas golf.

Eschenbrenner grew up in Fort Worth, where as a teenager he started caddying at Worth Hills Golf Course. Lovingly referred to as Goat Hills, the city-owned course near the campus of Texas Christian University was immortalized by Jenkins in a 1965 *Sports Illustrated* article titled "The Glory Game at Goat Hills."

Jenkins and his cohorts, who included a teenage Eschenbrenner, would play money games in gangs of as many as twenty players. The "holes" would start the way they were drawn up on the scorecard, but soon expand to cross-country voyages: from the second tee to the ninth green, for example, hitting across fairways and over trees.

They would even play across town. "We once played from the first tee at Goat Hills to the first green at Colonial Country Club," Esch says. "We played through a parking lot at TCU, through a vacant lot, right through a barbed-wire fence, and right through the Colonial members onto the first green. There were about ten of us."

Of course, Esch could play conventional golf pretty well, too. He won both the Fort Worth Junior City Championship and the men's City Championship. After graduating from my alma mater, the University of North Texas, in 1961, Esch went west to El Paso and became the head professional of El Paso Country Club in 1965. Since then, he has made numerous contributions to the area.

He helped start the golf program at the University of Texas-El Paso and also founded the Western Refining College All-America Golf Classic, one of the biggest tournaments in college golf. Held at El Paso Country Club, the event has boasted winners such as Tiger Woods, Davis Love III, Jerry Pate, and David Duval.

In addition to mentoring tour players such as Joel Edwards and Rich Beem, Esch was good friends with Lee Trevino and was the man responsible for helping Lee gain a PGA membership card so he could play on tour. Who knows? If not for Esch, Trevino might not have gotten his shot on tour. As it turned out, Trevino was one of the best ball-strikers ever, and I have no doubt Esch had a lot to do with that.

Esch also helped everyday players at El Paso. He leased the old, tired Cielo Vista Golf Course and converted it into the Lone Star Golf Course, a terrific municipal layout. In addition, he helped develop El Paso's junior golf program.

For a long time, I felt that Esch never received the attention and credit he deserved, partly because he lived and worked in a remote corner of west Texas. So I was ecstatic when he was recognized in 2005 as the PGA of America's Golf Professional of the Year.

I first met him in 1978 through my college roommate, Joel Edwards. Joel's family had been members at El Paso Country Club, and he grew up taking lessons from Esch.

Growing up in Minnesota, I was a big fish in a small pond. When I got to North Texas, I realized how much I needed to improve in order to achieve my goal of being a professional golfer. A large part of that realization was watching Joel on the range for the first time.

I had never seen anybody hit a golf ball as solidly as Joel did. The ball just rocketed off the face, flew laser-straight, and landed next to the flag he had been aiming at. I had never imagined that a golf shot could be hit that purely. And the amazing part was that he did it so consistently.

Joel and I became friends, and I soon learned that his teacher was Eschenbrenner. The next time Joel went to El Paso to see Esch, I asked to come along because I also wanted a lesson from the man who'd taught my friend how to hit the ball so squarely and reliably.

Joel arranged for us to spend the night at Bill's house, then go to the course early the following morning. We arrived late, and Esch couldn't have been more friendly and welcoming. We chatted a bit as he asked about my background and how I had come to enroll at North Texas.

But the following morning at the golf course, his manner was different. Although he was still friendly, it was clear that the driving range was his place of business. His job was helping golfers play better, and he took the task seriously.

A tough, no-nonsense teacher, Esch worked best with students willing to work hard to help themselves, because that is what he had done. When Esch spoke, he had a sense of credibility and authority because, like fellow Fort Worth native Ben Hogan, he had learned the game by digging it out of the dirt. Lee Trevino always said that he could never take a lesson from anyone who couldn't beat him. Esch was one of Trevino's mentors.

During my first lesson with him, Esch began to fix my position at impact. You can teach golf by working the big muscles. You can focus on small muscles of the hands and arms. You can teach by complicated mechanics or by feel and imagery. But no matter how you teach or how you learn, ultimately only one part of the swing truly matters: impact.

And I learned more about impact from Esch than I did from anyone else. All of his top students, especially Joel, had good impact positions. In the downswing, all of them had plenty of lag, which is the angle formed by the left arm and the shaft. The goal is to release this angle as late as possible in the downswing, so the hands are well ahead of the ball at impact. This position promotes a slightly downward path of the club in the downswing so the head hits the ball squarely, before the ground.

Releasing this angle too early in the downswing is known as casting, leading to an impact position in which the hands are behind the ball. This causes a scooping motion, leading to fat or thin shots. This is one of the most common faults in golf, and I never saw any of Esch's students scooping the ball with loose, cuppy wrists.

At impact, Esch wanted you to feel as if the clubhead was lagging behind so it pinched the ball. To practice this, Esch had me take my address position, then place the clubhead two feet behind the ball (away from the target). He then had me drag the club through the ball by pulling my left side. When I did it correctly, the sensation was that of effortless power.

Among today's players, the one who best emulates Esch's ideal impact position is Sergio Garcia. He has tremendous lag in the downswing, and his hands are well ahead of the ball at impact. It's no surprise that Garcia is one of the best ball-strikers in golf. If only he could make a few more putts, he would have won several majors in his first ten years on tour.

Lee Trevino's swing—marked by a weak left-hand grip, open stance, and rerouting from the backswing to the downswing—looks remarkably orthodox at impact. Trevino's motion shows us that no matter what else you do in the swing, it is the impact position that matters.

Another of Esch's students is Rich Beem, winner of the 2002 PGA Championship. Unlike Trevino, whose swing is rather flat, Beem has an upright motion. Although these two motions might be at the extremes of the swing plane, what they have in common is the position at impact: hands ahead and shaft leaning toward the target.

To achieve this impact position, Esch emphasizes the importance of having a firm left side: the legs, the torso, and especially the arm. This firmness stabilizes the swing and lets the hands get ahead of the ball.

What's interesting about the firm left side is that it places a lot of emphasis on the left hand and arm, since that hand has to pull the club through impact. I have no doubt that a big reason why Joel could get into such a good position is that he is left-handed. This strength in his left side allows him to control his swing better.

It's also fascinating to note that some other famous ball-strikers in history had stronger lead (facing the target) sides. Ben Hogan was left-handed; he even started playing from the other side of the ball as a beginner. And perhaps no player in history had a better impact position than Hogan.

Johnny Miller was another left-hander who played right-handed. And during the 1970s, he was the best iron player in the game, no doubt due to his impact position. For a stretch, Miller would consider it a bad shot if it finished twenty feet to the left or right of the hole.

And in today's era, the left-handed Phil Mickelson is actually a righty, who does everything else right-handed. He learned to play golf left-handed because, as a child, he used to watch his father, a righty, hit balls, and he started to mimic him as a mirror image. I think Mickelson hits the ball so well because he uses his dominant side to pull the clubhead through impact.

I'm not saying that you should play golf left-handed if you're a righty. But if you want to take a tip from Esch (or Hogan or Mickelson), pay more attention to the lead side in your golf swing. It will help your impact position.

No matter how you get there, impact is king. That is the lasting lesson I received from Bill Eschenbrenner, and it is a lesson I refer to nearly every day when I'm out there giving lessons and trying to help my students hit the ball straighter, longer, and more consistently.

MARK'S LESSONS

There is a strong correlation between impact position and skill level. That shouldn't come as a surprise, since position has a direct effect on how the ball travels: The better the impact position, the straighter and farther the ball will fly.

In fact, all I really need to determine a golfer's general skill level is to look at a photo of his or her impact position. While there are many different body parts to examine at impact—weight transfer, spine angle, head position—there is one constant among all the best players: hand position.

The lower your handicap and the better ball-striker you are, the closer your hands are to the target at impact.

Keeping the hands ahead of the ball has many benefits. It promotes a downward angle of attack so the clubhead meets the ball before the ground. It makes sure the clubface is square so you make solid contact instead of cutting across the ball with a glancing blow. Finally, it leans the shaft forward and delofts the clubface. So that seven-iron effectively becomes a six-iron or even a five-iron, enabling you to hit the ball longer. Here are some tips for improving your impact position.

HIGH HANDICAPPER

The impact position is largely a product of what happens beforehand, namely the transition from the backswing to the downswing. In his *Little Red Book,* Harvey refers to this first part of the downswing as the "Magic Move."

To help your impact position, try rehearsing this move the way Harvey described it: "To start your downswing, let your weight shift to your left foot [for a right-hander] while bringing your right elbow back down to your body. This is one move, not two. Practice this move again and again. You don't need a golf club to do it. Practice until you get the feeling and rhythm of it, and then keep on practicing."

MID HANDICAPPER

The best way to groove a hands-ahead impact position is to feel the move without a ball, since trying to hit the ball is what causes the hands to be too far behind it at impact. The idea is to swing through the ball, not at it.

Make swings against an impact bag or a tire. You'll find that impact will hurt unless your hands are ahead of the clubhead.

Another good drill is to set the clubhead at least one foot behind the ball, along the target line but on the side opposite the target. Then pull the club forward so the clubhead stays along the ground and drags through the ball.

One foot

LOW HANDICAPPER

The one aspect of impact that separates a good amateur from a professional is how long the clubhead travels along the target line while the clubface remains square.

The good amateur's clubhead comes from inside the target line in the downswing and moves back inside following impact; so that from above, the club moves in an arc, similar to a windshield wiper. That is the result of flipping the club through impact with the hands and requires perfect timing to hit straight shots.

Low-handicap players are good enough to square the club most of the time, but they hit their share of off-line shots if their timing is off. The beauty of the tour swing is that because there is little timing involved, the shots are much more consistent.

Amateur

Rich Beem is one of the best I have seen at keeping the clubhead moving down the line. While most players, even tour pros, start their divots just ahead of the ball, Beem's divots start a couple of inches in front of the ball—that shows how square the club is through impact. As a result, Beem hits the ball dead straight, with little curve.

The lesson here is to work on releasing the club more with the body and less with the hands. The more you can keep the hands out of the swing, the more forward your hands will be at impact and the longer you will keep the clubhead and clubface square through the hitting zone.

Professional

BOBBY LOCKE

The Joy of Putting

In January 1983, I traveled to South Africa to play the Sunshine Tour. At the time, I was trying to decide between playing and teaching. I was working at Denton Country Club, and my boss, Frank Jennings, wanted me to give playing a shot. He made a deal with me: I would go to South Africa for three months and compete. If I didn't like it, my job would be waiting upon my return. At the time, there were fewer venues for aspiring tour pros. I could have gone to Florida to play the mini-tours, but I didn't want to pay high entry fees that went to pay for prize money, ride carts without caddies, and play two-round events.

Then as now, the Sunshine Tour was one of the major worldwide tours that attracted strong fields, especially in the winter (their summer), while the PGA and European tours were on hiatus. Everything was first-class: You had to have a caddie, all the events were four rounds with a cut after two rounds (players making the cut were exempt for the following week), and the final two rounds were televised.

I knew before I left that the Sunshine Tour was competitive, but I was still surprised by the skill level of the players. Southern Africa has produced some really fine players: major championship winners Bobby Locke, Gary Player, Nick Price, Ernie Els, and Trevor Immelman.

During my three months, the fields on the Sunshine Tour included not only Player and Price, but also David Frost, Denis Watson, Mark McNulty, and Fulton Allem, all of whom became top players in America or Europe. In addition, there were other young Americans testing their games, including

Bob Tway and Corey Pavin, who won the South African PGA Championship, one of the tour's three majors, along with the South African Open and South African Masters.

Of course when I arrived in South Africa and started playing, I had no idea that I was competing with future PGA Tour champions. All I knew was that these guys were really, really good.

Traveling halfway around the world was a daunting prospect, but I needed to put myself in the position of being a small fish in a big pond if I was going to grow as a person, a player, and a teacher. Thankfully, I had an experienced travel partner: North Texas alumnus Jimmy Johnson, who knew a lot of the players and later wound up caddying for Price.

I arrived in Johannesburg and qualified the next day for my first tournament at the Wanderers Golf Club. After a practice round, I was working on my putting stroke on the practice green, wearing the style of flat hat that Ben Hogan made popular and which soon came to be named for him. A heavyset man and his wife came over and introduced themselves.

I was so into my putting that I missed their names; I thought they were members of the club and were being friendly. But instead of taking a hint from my lack of interest, the man kept talking to me. He asked, "Are you from the States?"

I told him that I was from the Dallas/Fort Worth area of Texas, and he seemed interested that I was from "Hogan Country," as he put it, and also noted that I was wearing a Hogan-style cap. He said that he had been to the United States to play golf, mentioning especially that he loved American beer.

The man talked about some of the courses he had played. It seemed like he was well connected, considering he had played some of the best courses in the country, including Augusta National Golf Club.

The conversation then turned to my putting, which was poor at the time. He became very animated. He said he loved to putt, no matter the condition of the greens, and that nothing gave him more pleasure than making putts against his opponents. I assumed he was talking about club matches.

He laughed a lot and he didn't seem to take himself too seriously. In fact, my initial reluctance had disappeared, and I found myself enjoying our conversation. I had never met anyone who enjoyed talking about a subject as much as this man did when he discussed putting. I was having trouble on the greens and was really down on myself, and it clearly showed in my words and demeanor. The man tried to help me relax and understand that missing a putt wasn't life and death. His laughter, jovial outlook, and round belly reminded me of Santa Claus.

After a while, he finally got me to understand that I was trying too hard. I had always thought that intensity and focus were good things. I now realized that my approach was hurting me because every missed putt was affecting my outlook.

By now, it was time for tea and scones, a mid afternoon tradition at South African clubs. He invited me up to the clubhouse to join him and his wife. On the way inside, I thought it was odd that everyone we passed—players, caddies, spectators—stopped to greet him. He seemed to be a popular member indeed.

We sat down and continued our conversation. I *really* began to wonder who this man was when Gary Player came over to our table and started talking to him as if he were an old friend. It was my first week in the country, and I had somehow wound up sitting with the most popular man in South African golf.

As Player walked away, I decided that I needed to find out who my new best friend was. The problem was that after an hour of talking to the man, I couldn't just ask for his name. Luckily, Don Robertson, my traveling partner, came over and whispered in my ear, "How did you wind up sitting with Bobby Locke?"

I was dumbfounded. Bobby Locke was the first great South African champion, the winner of four British Opens, and one of the greatest putters of all time. The matches he had mentioned were no mere club events: They were with the best players in the world, including Sam Snead, against whom he won twelve of fourteen matches in a series of exhibitions.

And Locke's golf tour of the United States was no mere holiday. He'd played on the PGA Tour for three seasons, from 1947 to 1949, and won eleven of fifty-nine events. He also finished second ten times, third eight times, and fourth five times. In fact, he was so good that the other players began to resent that he was taking so much money out of their pockets and the tour found a way to ban him on a technicality.

Although the ban was later lifted, Locke didn't feel welcome and never returned to play in the United States full-time. Thirty years later, those ill feelings seemed to be gone as he welcomed an American from Texas and spoke warmly about his time in the States.

In that first meeting with Locke, he taught me a lot about putting. I wouldn't say he had a great stroke, technique-wise. He used a lot of wrist action, and the path of his putter head came into impact extremely from the inside. It certainly wasn't a stroke that I would teach to my students. But Locke had grooved his stroke and he had confidence.

It was Locke's mental approach that made him a great putter. During all his talk about putting, he never mentioned his misses; he only referred to the putts he had made. It wasn't that he never missed; he knew that lingering thoughts over the bad putts had no place in his psyche. He wanted to make putting enjoyable, and there is no greater way to do that than to recall all your good putts.

I think of that every time I see a tour pro with a grim intensity on his face before a putt and a disapproving look after a miss. I came away from my encounter with Locke with a new approach to putting. Afterward, I stopped treating every putt as if it were as serious as surgery, and tried to focus on all the positive aspects of putting. Locke was known for telling people that he could roll the ball over peanut brittle.

Also, I had met so many people while with Locke that I immediately felt more comfortable in such an unfamiliar place. Although he had been retired from competition for years, he was still a very popular figure in South African golf, and for the next three months, many players knew me as Bobby Locke's friend with the Hogan hat.

Despite the revelations about my putting, my time in South Africa taught me that my golf future was in teaching, not playing. Foremost, my experience playing on the Sunshine Tour lifted me out of my comfort zone. Improvement in golf comes from challenging yourself at higher levels and competing with better players.

There are plenty of weekend golfers who only play with buddies in casual rounds in which the phrase "That's good" is uttered far too often. These players should play matches or events that require them to putt everything out. Even an eighteen-inch putt is no gimme when you have to make it for par.

At the next level, good club players should enter local tournaments to test their games both against other good amateurs and on different courses. After shooting an 83 that exposed your inability to hit fairways, you may be surprised to find out that what enabled you to shoot 72 regularly on your home course has more to do with your familiarity with the layout than with your skill.

I had similar revelations while competing against players on the Sunshine Tour who would go on to be among the best in the world. One of these occurred on the practice tee before rounds. At the time, players would warm up by hitting balls not on a range but on a field. They would hit balls to their caddies, who would either catch the ball on a fly or scoop it up after the ball landed and came to a dead stop.

This was my first exposure to this type of practice session, and I thought it was a bit bizarre. But I still had to warm up before my round, and after hitting a few tentative wedges to my caddie, I started working my way through the bag, hitting progressively longer clubs. I quickly noticed that my caddie reacted differently to my shots. Instead of standing his ground as my shots came down the way the other caddies would, he would always back up, picking up the ball after two or three hops, like a baseball shortstop fielding ground balls.

The big difference between the way I hit my shots and the way the other players hit theirs was spin. The other players hit their shots with a lot more spin, which enabled the ball to land softer and stay put, whereas my shots had less spin, which meant the balls would bounce uncontrollably after hitting the ground. Ultimately, the other players had much better control of their shots than I did.

I realized that this control was the result of striking the ball with a consistent angle of attack that allowed the ball to climb up the clubface slightly before leaving the face. To this day, I work on controlling spin, which is the key to controlling trajectory and distance.

Revelations like these excited the teacher in me, and I found myself studying these great players. It was more fun for me to watch Gary Player hitting bunker shots than it was hitting the shots myself. I learned how he made adjustments in his clubface, stance, and swing to control his shots. I was also entranced by watching a young Nick Price hitting iron shots. Nick later became the best ball-striker in golf, but even back then, the way he hit the ball was so pure that it stood out from the field.

Eventually, I learned how to play golf and get the ball in the hole, instead of just execute good shots. During a round, I would feel like I had hit the ball much better than my playing partner, but when we added up our scores at the end, he would have beaten me by several strokes.

I realized that playing good golf had a lot more to do with my mental approach than I ever had thought. While I would get upset over a poor shot and let that feeling linger for a while, which affected my next shot, my partners would be able to shrug it off and make a great recovery for par.

Harvey always told me that you learn how to play from players, how to teach from teachers, and how to coach from coaches. After getting an up-close look at players like Bobby Locke and Nick Price and getting inside their heads, I had received lessons I never would have gotten otherwise.

While you may never join the Sunshine Tour, putting yourself in unfamiliar situations can help your golf game. Complacency is never a good formula for improvement.

MARK'S LESSONS

Putting is a game within a game. It requires a different set of skills—both physically and mentally—than making a golf swing. It is often the difference between a good player and a great player, and it can be the equalizer for someone who isn't a great ball-striker.

That certainly was the case for Locke, who probably looked forward to putting more than any other player in golf history. His full swing, which produced low hooks with every club in the bag, was just a prelude, a way to get the ball on the green, where the game really began for him.

His approach was the dead opposite of Ben Hogan's. For Hogan, the real appeal of golf was in the tee-to-green game, and he worked hard to hone his swing because he enjoyed it so much. On the green, Hogan just didn't have the same cool demeanor. "There is no similarity between golf and putting," Hogan once said. "They are two different games, one played in the air, and the other on the ground." Because Hogan was such a great ball-striker, he won events despite his average putting, but he could have won more majors, most notably the 1960 U.S. Open, if he had made some more putts.

The great part of this division between the full swing and the putting stroke is that anybody can be a good putter. If you want to lower your scores, the quickest way is to improve your putting. It doesn't take a superhuman effort to average thirty-six putts a round—that's just two putts per green. But most amateurs probably take at least forty putts per round, which means there is a pretty big margin for improvement.

The first step is to adopt Locke's joyful approach to putting. The second is to incorporate the following tips.

HIGH HANDICAPPER

Most high-handicap golfers have more three-putt greens than two-putt greens. Why? Their lag putting is horrible. From twenty feet and out, they rarely hit their first putts into tap-in range.

To improve your lag putting and cut down drastically on your number of three-putts, focus on two things: making solid contact and pace, not direction.

While making solid contact may seem obvious, it's often overlooked when players analyze their putting woes. Just as off-center hits hurt distance off the tee, the same thing happens on the green. If you consistently leave long putts short, focus on making contact on the putter's sweet spot. You can do that by keeping your body still during the stroke (it's amazing how many people move during the putting motion) and accelerating the putter through impact with a square path. Decelerating or cutting across the ball are common faults.

I also find that most golfers focus too much on the line and not enough on the speed of the putt. Even if you significantly misread a putt but hit the ball at the right pace, it will end up two feet left or right of the hole—a very feasible distance. But mistakes in pace can leave you as much as ten feet short of the hole or behind it, and you can't reasonably expect to make putts that are that long.

So don't worry so much about the line and spend most of your pre-putt routine on getting the pace right, especially as the putts get longer.

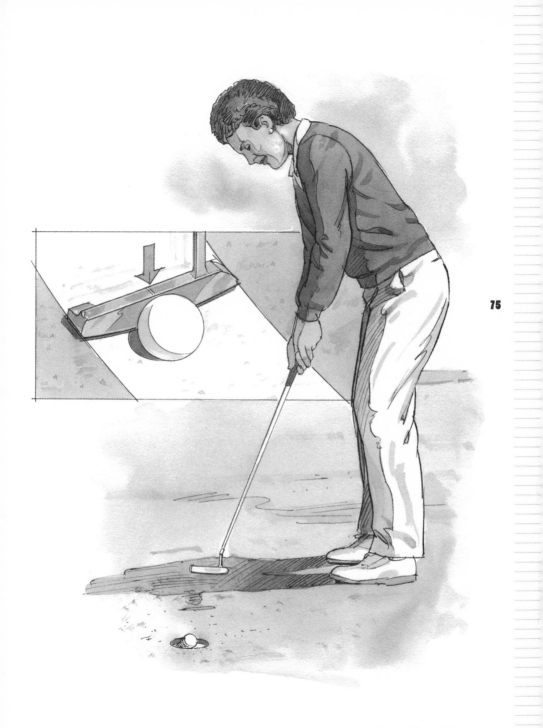

MID HANDICAPPER

As the distance of your putts gets shorter, the line becomes more important, and the key is in melding the two properly to make more putts, whether for birdie, par, or bogey.

While the line is important, it is related to speed. I always find it amusing when a caddie I have just met authoritively gives me the line to a ten-foot putt on the first green. "One ball out on the right," he'll say without a hint of doubt in his voice. How does he know that when he doesn't know how hard I like to hit my putts? If I like to hit putts with a lot of pace so that if they miss they wind up three feet behind the hole, they will break less. If I prefer to die putts into the hole, there will be more break.

So it is important to decide first how hard you want to hit the putt, before determining the line. That will help you hole more achievable putts from ten feet and in.

LOW HANDICAPPER

At the higher levels of the game, it's good to make birdies. But it's imperative not to make bogeys and especially double bogeys. While it's nice to make a six-foot birdie putt, missing it won't hurt your scorecard. The same can't be said for a par putt of the same length.

A crucial par putt can buoy your round by making up for a mistake that put you in potential trouble. Chances are, you are facing this sort of par putt because you missed a green and have to chip or pitch toward the hole.

You can use this as an opportunity to leave yourself a high-percentage putt. While you can't necessarily control where an iron shot ends up, you can do so with pitches and chips. The easiest putts are those with less break or those that are uphill, so try to favor that side of the hole. Keep in mind that an uphill, right-to-left, eight-foot putt is easier to make than a downhill, left-to-right putt from four feet, so leave yourself the most doable putt possible. It will give you more confidence as you make that important round-saving par.

DAVE PELZ

Dave Pelz's scientific approach has lifted the entire teaching industry, and during my years at the Academy of Golf in the early eighties, I had the privilege of watching him develop his teaching philosophies as he gathered data on thousands of shots.

When you're analyzing your game, it is easy to come to conclusions based on perception. For an objective assessment, there is no simpler way than to keep track of your fairways hit, greens hit, and putts per round.

You may think you're a good putter, but if you average more than thirty-six putts per round, you need to spend time on the practice green.

HARVEY PENICK

The Best Lesson

I n addition to giving thousands of lessons during my career, I have
watched hundreds of lessons. The instructors have ranged from apprentices
to master PGA professionals who have been teaching for decades. The students
have ranged from beginners who had never before held a club to tour pros who
were trying to turn a ten-yard draw into a five-yard curve.

Every golfer has a different approach to learning the game, and the most
effective lessons are the ones in which the teacher's method matches the student's learning style. Harvey Penick could make that judgment after talking
to a new student for just a few minutes.

He made a lot of determinations based on his analysis of the golfer's hands.
He noticed whether you had long or short fingers, big or little palms, and where
your club was positioned in your hands. At your first lesson with Harvey, you
didn't wear gloves. He thought that with gloves, students could fool themselves
into taking a grip that looked okay but couldn't perform properly.

Harvey believed that the grip affected clubface angle, bottom of the arc,
and even balance. In fact, some of Harvey's lessons never advanced beyond
the grip. Other times, it never got beyond Harvey watching the student hitting a few balls.

As his fame grew, people started offering a lot of money for Harvey's
lessons, but he always said that he couldn't charge big dollars for little
lessons. Harvey used simple words, even when the student was looking for
lessons that included more in-depth information. One of the best examples of
Harvey's teaching prowess was a lesson he gave at Austin Country Club that,

of all the sessions I have given or watched, stands out in my mind as the best lesson ever given.

This student had an analytical mind and came to the lesson with enough swing theories to fill a thousand-page book. He told Harvey all about his history in the game and all the lessons he had taken from all the other teachers he had seen. He talked about all the approaches and philosophies he had tried over the decades.

Harvey barely said a word, just nodding. Clearly, every instructor this student had hired had picked up on his studious nature and given him plenty of analytic thoughts for his swing.

After a while, Harvey asked the man to hit some balls. After a few swings, it didn't take an expert to see that this man was truly lost. He hit the first shot fairly well, but that was his last good shot. He hit his second shot fat and began setting up for his third swing. He looked tense, like he was struggling to recite a checklist of steps.

It came as no surprise that he started hitting balls in all directions. He would hit one ball left, make a compensation before the next swing, then hit the next shot the other way. With so many thoughts in his head, he had no pattern to his misses.

As the man's frustration began to build, Harvey just kept quiet. After fifteen or so shots, no two alike, I knew Harvey was ready to start his lesson. I couldn't wait to hear what the master had to say.

As I watched, I was focusing on the mechanics of the man's swing. Which part should he work on first? The grip? The balance? The bottom of the arc? What would Harvey advise? I expected a little anecdote and a drill or simple instruction. I did not expect what came next.

Before the next swing, Harvey used a rather forceful voice (Harvey was usually soft-spoken) to tell the man simply to concentrate on keeping his eye on the ball. And not just the ball, but rather a specific part: the dot of the "i" in Maxfli.

The man was confused. He was used to hearing terms such as "pronation," "swing plane," "weight transfer," and "release." No doubt, he was expecting to hear a lengthy dissection of his swing or at least a thought that had to do with his motion. But he had come a long way to see Harvey, and he listened despite his disappointment.

He hit the next shot fairly solidly, and Harvey repeated his directive. In fact, he just said the same thing after every shot. And remarkably, the man started to hit the ball quite well. The tension—both physical and mental—was gone from his swing as he followed Harvey's instruction.

I was surprised. This man was as analytical as any golfer I had ever met, and here he was, hitting good shots from advice that beginners give to each other because they don't know anything else to say about the golf swing.

At the end of the thirty-minute lesson, the man was hitting the ball better than he ever had in his life, and he couldn't have been happier. He thanked Harvey many times and left the range as content as if he had won the U.S. Open.

The man had barely picked up his clubs when I walked up to Harvey and asked him why he had given this piece of advice to the man. Harvey admitted that "Keep your eye on the ball" in itself was useless to the man; after all, it wasn't as if the man's fault was that he was moving his head too much.

Harvey went on to say that this man had a lot of swing thoughts running through his head—a classic case of "paralysis by analysis." He told me that what you say to your student is going to be his or her main thought over the ball, and the teacher has to be careful about how he presents this information.

Harvey easily could have given this man a swing thought that was related to his fault. But he realized that given the man's nature, he would have over-interpreted the thought and it would have done more harm than good. So Harvey placed the man's train of thought on a new track. He had never before simply focused on the ball, and doing so enabled him finally to make swings free of a debilitating sea of thoughts.

Since then, whenever I give a lesson, I try to explore all the ways I can help the student, to find the best one for that individual, even if it may not seem to fit what the student perceives as his or her learning style.

MARK'S LESSONS

The lesson I described was classic Harvey—simple yet incredibly insightful. Recalling that day led me to thinking about some of the best lessons that I have given. Hopefully you will be able to learn a little something from them.

HIGH HANDICAPPER

By far, the most common fault I see among high handicappers is a slice. And most people slice because they can't square the clubface through impact. Sometimes it's because of physical limitations. Other times it's because they don't have the correct feel or image.

I once gave a lesson to a beginner who had trouble with a slice. No matter how I explained the swing, he couldn't release the club properly. Then I found out that he was a former baseball player.

So I had him imagine that he was at bat on a baseball field. And I told him that as he swung, he should try to hit a line drive over the shortstop's head. That got him to roll the forearms and close the face. He could relate to that image, and it helped him cure his slice.

MID HANDICAPPER

While I was at the Academy of Golf in Austin, Texas, I gave a lesson to a man from Houston who hit the ball everywhere. He hit some good shots and made some pars, but he made so many big numbers that he couldn't get his score down.

There wasn't much wrong with his swing, so I suggested we go play a few holes. On the first hole, a long par-four, I told him to divide the hole into three par-threes.

Off the tee, instead of hitting a driver, he used a four-wood. He hit the fairway. On the next shot, I told him to imagine a target about 150 yards away and once again play it as a par-three. He hit a good seven-iron, which left him about 110 yards from the green. The final par-three was a short one, and he hit a pitching wedge onto the green. He nearly made par.

We played the rest of the nine this way, and it was remarkable how much he played under control. He made all pars and bogeys—not a single double. This was one of the first non-mechanics-related lessons I gave, and it helped him lower his handicap significantly.

LOW HANDICAPPER

Even good players have trouble with sand. They may be able to get out, but many golfers don't know how to control the distance of the shot. Once, I had a four-handicap who was trying to get to scratch, but his bunker paly was holding him back. It was an automatic bogey every time his ball found the sand.

His setup was good, but the shape of his swing was too steep. He would hit low, running shots that rarely stopped close to the hole. He knew that his swing was supposed to be shallow, but his desire to dig into the sand and extricate the ball overcame any sense of logic.

So after a while, I buried a piece of wood under the sand, placed a ball on top of the board, and had him hit a shot. There was a loud *thwack* as the wedge hit the wood solidly. Based on how loud the impact was, I'm sure it hurt quite a bit.

After asking whether he was all right (he was), I instructed him to keep hitting balls with the board buried under the sand until the sound became muffled and the bottom of the sand wedge bounced off the sand as if he were skipping rocks on water.

Based on this sound feedback, he learned to shallow out his swing and hit high, soft shots that allowed him to control the distance. He could get up and down for par more often than not. He no longer dreaded the sand, and when he hit an iron shot into a green off-line, he could be found yelling at the ball "Get in the sand!"

**MIKE ADAMS, BILL MORETTI,
MIKE McGETRICK**

The Academy Years

I n 1987, life was pretty good for me. I was working at the North Texas State University golf course in Denton, Texas. I had a stable group of students who were improving steadily, and I was developing a successful junior program.

In addition I had gotten married the year before, and my wife, Lisa, had just been hired to teach first grade at a new school in town. And we had just bought our first house.

Denton was a nice city on the fringes of the Dallas/Forth Worth metroplex. It was far enough north of Dallas to feel a bit more relaxed, yet close enough to enjoy the city's attractions.

It was a great place to start our lives together, and it would have been ridiculous to upset that. So of course I did just that, by taking a job at the Academy of Golf, located at the Hills of Lakeway in Austin.

It wasn't an easy decision, but in the end, it came down to being able to teach full time and being able to move to Austin, where I could visit Harvey Penick regularly instead of just every other month or so.

So I moved to Austin in January, while Lisa stayed in Denton so she could finish out the school year. This isn't a move I would recommend to other newlyweds, but Lisa was understanding, and it turned out to be a wise decision for both of us.

The Academy of Golf was a great place for a young teacher to hone his craft. In addition to working alongside other talented beginning teachers, I learned a lot about instruction from the owners, Mike Adams and Bill Moretti.

Mike has one of the best golf minds I have ever encountered. He lives and breathes golf instruction, and his passion for the subject is so great that he never tires of speaking about it, whether he is talking with a tour pro, a fellow teacher, or a high handicapper.

His energy is infectious, and those who spend time with him can't help but be pulled along. In those early days, he would regularly host a bunch of us at his house, and we would spend hours discussing instruction.

This constant immersion in the subject was perfect for somebody like me, who was relatively new to the business. Mike showed me that no matter how much you know about the golf swing, there is no substitute for passion and love of the game when it comes to reaching students.

While Bill didn't have Mike's outsize personality, the pair complemented each other well. Mike was the front man for the Academy, but Bill was more low-key. He had worked for David Leadbetter for several years before moving to Austin. He was more studious than Mike and could diagnose any fault and prescribe a fix in two seconds.

A lot of what the two of them said simply went over my head at first, but I asked a lot of questions. For a student used to receiving simplified but highly effective bromides from Harvey Penick, Mike and Bill's conversations about the technical causes and effects of the swing were a real eye-opener.

The third man in the organization was Mike McGetrick, who was a master of the behind-the-scenes details. He administered and planned our golf schools to perfection. When the students arrived, they were amazed by how well organized and efficient the sessions were. And thanks in large part to McGetrick, the sessions were always productive.

McGetrick was also technically oriented and was responsible for our video systems. Nowadays, video is an integral component in an instructor's toolbox. But nearly twenty-five years ago, few teachers used it, and McGetrick knew more about the systems than most other teachers at the time.

Mike is my age, and we got along very well together. He has a warm personality, and truly cared for his students above and beyond the lessons themselves. He spent a lot of time getting to know them, so he could have a better idea of how to motivate them and so they could get the most out of their practice time. Golf instruction was far more than a business to him.

After leaving the Academy of Golf, Mike went on to teach top LPGA players such as Juli Inkster, Meg Mallon, and Beth Daniel.

There was a lot of teaching talent under one roof at the Academy. On top of that, Dave Pelz opened a school on the same driving range. Pelz was just starting his short-game schools, and this was back when he was still gathering all the data that became the foundation for his teaching philosophies and ideas. More so than any other teacher before or since, Pelz studied how people hit shots (and miss them); he made golf instruction a left-brain activity.

All together, the Academy was a living laboratory of golf instruction. We saw more than two thousand students each year; and I quickly learned what Harvey meant when he used to say, "We teach people to play golf, not golf to people." There was no one-size-fits-all approach, even when teaching at a golf school with a student-teacher ratio of six to one.

For example, I might have trouble with a student who couldn't stop coming over the top. No matter how I tried, I wasn't getting through. But Adams and Moretti were able to help the student because of their experience. They had learned different ways of saying the same thing, and I was impressed by their ability to communicate.

A lot of their experience, and some of mine, came from the Academy's role as a practice facility for the University of Texas golf team. We saw a lot of really good golfers during their college years, and it was my first real exposure to teaching top players. I figured these guys would be able to take a piece of advice and incorporate it into their swing without a second thought. It wasn't so.

Even future tour pros like Bob Estes and Justin Leonard clicked better with some instructors than with others. When it came down to it, we weren't really teaching golf; we were trying to connect with each of our students. The teaching and learning process depends heavily on the personalities involved, and the best teachers seem able to adapt to their students.

An initial lesson during which a teacher and student don't connect is like a bad first date. Pelz and Gary Hallberg were a perfect example. As I said earlier, Pelz brought a cerebral approach to instruction, and Hallberg relied heavily on feel.

Hallberg never thought about the golf swing; he just played. That approach made him a great amateur—at Wake Forest he was the first player to be named first-team All-America all four years. When he turned pro in 1980, he made enough money in a few events to earn a PGA Tour card for the following year instead of going to Qualifying School, the same way Leonard and Tiger Woods did years later.

Feel players are hard to teach because they don't respond well to technical analysis like, "Lay the club off a bit at the top of the backswing to prevent a hook." That's why, as I described in a previous chapter, Harvey took Ben Crenshaw, a feel player, to a corner of the range next to a hole and had him hit drives that stayed out of the fairway so he would stop hooking.

Pelz couldn't do that with Hallberg. A former NASA engineer, Pelz only knew how to relay precise information and instructions, which were a foreign language to Hallberg. After months of working together, they eventually parted ways.

Another revelatory experience in my time at the Academy was taking part in a national PGA Junior golf camp with twelve or so excellent teachers from around the country. The biggest lesson I took away from that was how different each of their teaching styles was. No two were alike!

One instructor was talking about the second spine angle, which seemed to confuse the kids, who no doubt played their best with simpler thoughts in their heads. Other instructors were using different drills to get their points across, sometimes with contradictory results.

Individually, each of these teachers knew a lot about the swing and the game, and no doubt could teach each of the juniors something in a one-on-one setting. But in a group environment, the combined knowledge did more harm than good, in my opinion. Instead of keeping things simple, we were making the game more complicated.

As a young teacher just learning about the business, I found it all dizzying. But at the same time, being exposed to so many different methods helped me crystallize my own philosophy.

So I began to forge my own path and gain confidence in my own methods. And what I agreed with wasn't necessarily the approach espoused by the biggest names in the teaching business. With each passing day, I felt more and more like a baseball umpire making a call and knowing it was the right one.

I acquired this confidence and maturity while working at the Academy. Harvey inspired me to become a golf instructor. My colleagues at the Academy honed that desire into sharp skills that I can apply to any situation. And should I ever have any questions or problems, I can still call Mike Adams, Mike McGetrick, or Bill Moretti and ask for advice.

This type of network is invaluable for a teacher, and my years at the Academy helped me in more than my career. My experience there gave me long-lasting friendships.

MARK'S LESSONS

There are a lot of different ways to learn and play the game of golf. The hard part for average golfers is to find what fits their games and what doesn't. Most of us don't have the means to take private lessons from top instructors, so here are some tips to make your learning curve—and your game—more efficient.

HIGH HANDICAPPER

Focus on your short game. No matter your skill level, it is the quickest path to lower scores. It doesn't take much to hit a pitch or chip on the green in one shot, or to two-putt from twenty feet. But the inability to hit those seemingly simple shots consistently is the biggest factor in raising your score.

95

MID HANDICAPPER

As you get better, your distinct golf personality will start to emerge. You will discover your strengths and weaknesses, your predominant shot pattern, and your tendencies in certain situations. Start tailoring your play to match your strengths and avoid your weaknesses.

I like to compare this process to that of finding your position on a basketball team. If you're quick and a good dribbler, you'll be a point guard. If you're a good rebounder, you'll play in the paint as a forward.

While there are no positions in golf, there are different strategies. For example, if you predominantly hook the ball and you're playing a hole with water all the way down the left side, you should use a three-wood, which will have less sidespin than a driver. If you're a short hitter, you are better off playing a long par-four as a par-five, laying up and trying to hit a wedge close to the hole to make par instead of going for the green with a wood and getting into trouble.

LOW HANDICAPPER

As your scores come down, you expect to hit far more good shots than poor ones. But when you do hit a bad shot, the tendency is to linger over it in an attempt to analyze what went wrong and fix the fault for the next swing.

Unfortunately, dwelling on mechanics can lead to a downward spiral in your game. Tour pros rarely try to fix their swings while playing. Instead, they try to shoot the lowest scores possible with the swings they have brought to the course. In other words, they play golf instead of playing golf swing. If you stop self-critiquing, your mind can focus on the ultimate goal: Get the ball in the hole with the fewest possible strokes.

I find it interesting that while amateurs, even good ones, rarely hit balls after the round, tour pros do so all the time. What they're doing is figuring out what went wrong and how to fix it, so they'll return the next day with more confidence. Take a tip from them and work on your mechanics after the round, not during it.

DAVID FROST

I befriended David Frost during my time on South Africa's Sunshine Tour. Several years later, I caddied for him during a U.S. Open qualifying round. On several holes—the par-fives and on a par-four—he faced shots of about 240 to 250 yards.

Each time, I was tempted to hand him the three-wood, but he reached for the iron and laid up fifty yards short of the green. He got up and down every time. David knew that he was a better player with a wedge than with a fairway wood.

Too few amateurs are aware of their strengths and limitations the way tour pros are. They take risks, thinking of the glories of that once-in-a-lifetime shot they hit over water instead of the hundreds of other shots that fell short.

So when you make on-course decisions, take a lesson from David Frost and hit the shots that you can pull off consistently.

DR. JIM SUTTIE

The Mad Scientist

What's great about golf is that players of all sizes can be champions. Major winners range from five-foot-three Ian Woosnam to six-foot-seven George Archer, from 140-pound Corey Pavin to Craig Stadler, who didn't earn his nickname, "the Walrus," because he was as skinny as an eel.

Pavin and Stadler can't swing the same way. Their different body shapes won't let them, which is where Dr. Jim Suttie enters the picture.

Nobody I know has studied the golf swing as much as "Doc" has. Doc has all the latest electronic equipment to help him, and he has the largest collection of film and video of any instructor I know. When it comes to using gadgets, Dr. Suttie is at the opposite end of the spectrum from Harvey Penick, who employed nothing but his eyes. Doc uses sophisticated video-analysis software to study the swing, in addition to the same launch monitor used by the equipment companies and most sophisticated club-fitting services. He also uses high-speed cameras to study the putting stroke, and of course he offers lessons over the Internet.

Doc was chosen as the PGA of America's Teacher of the Year in 2000, and there is nothing that he doesn't know about the golf swing, accumulated over decades of research. He has taped the golf swing from all different angles, and he has the swings of all kinds of golfers, from tour pros to beginners, in his considerable database. If you're the analytic sort who likes a lot of information, no teacher is better for you than Doc.

With a doctorate in biomechanics, he has an edge when it comes to understanding how the body interacts with the golf club during the swing. He believes there are many different ways to swing a golf club successfully, based on your build, flexibility, timing attributes, and ball-flight preference.

I met Doc through Mike Adams while I was working at the Academy of Golf. Doc made several visits, and I always looked forward to discussing the physics of the golf swing with him. But I didn't understand the full scope of Doc's expertise until I worked with him at a golf school he was giving for his members at Medinah Country Club, located outside Chicago.

Jim was doing full-swing video analysis, and my job was to make sure the students were practicing what Doc wanted them to focus on. As the follow-up guy, I felt like an intern performing rounds at a hospital—an apt analogy, since I was working with a Doc.

Like any young doctor, I was eager to compare my diagnoses with those of the expert. Based on my experiences at previous schools, I expected Jim to spend about five minutes with each student—ten minutes at a maximum. But Doc spent about twenty to thirty minutes per student.

It was my first indication of how thorough and precise an instructor he was. It didn't matter that there was a large group in this school and that we were way behind schedule. Nothing was going to keep Doc from making the correct diagnosis. After all, he knew that making the wrong diagnosis could hurt the students who had put their trust in his expertise.

Dr. Suttie doesn't just look at what the club and body are doing during the swing. He goes beyond the surface to the player's fundamental physical characteristics, swing tendencies, and shot patterns.

For example, if a student is more comfortable with a strong grip, Jim won't recommend a forward ball position or upright swing path, both of which are incompatible with that grip. Or if a player has quick hands, Jim will work to build a swing that activates the small muscles.

Doc wants to avoid what he calls "mismatches." If a player has a strong grip, the last thing an instructor should do is ask that player to keep his or her legs quiet for better control. This prescription would take the power out of that particular player's swing.

Instead, Dr. Suttie wants "matching swing elements." These elements are different for every golfer, and it takes a while to get to the heart of what each student needs. That is why he took such a long time with each video diagnosis at the school where we worked together. When asked about his teaching philosophy, Doc responds: "No one swing fits all, but each person has his own perfect swing."

The best example of Suttie's genius was the work he did with Paul Azinger. The 1993 PGA Championship winner and 2008 Ryder Cup captain started playing golf seriously as a teenager—a relatively late bloomer. As a senior in high school, Azinger couldn't break 80 regularly.

He had never had a lesson when he went to see Doc. Most teachers would have started by overhauling Azinger's homemade swing, which consisted of an extremely strong grip, a short, flat backswing, and an aggressive leg-drive action through impact to stave off a hook. Rather than try to change Azinger's grip and swing action, Suttie encouraged him to work with his natural tendencies, which would be easier to hone, require fewer compensations, and perform more reliably under pressure.

If Azinger had tried to make his swing more orthodox, there's a good chance we never would have heard of him. And Doc knew it.

For every champion such as Sam Snead, Nick Faldo, and Tiger Woods, who developed "model" swings, there have been plenty more with idiosyncrasies that the average instructor would be tempted to fix.

Bobby Jones had a backswing that was nearly as long as John Daly's motion. Through impact, Byron Nelson had a pronounced dip with his legs. Jack Nicklaus had a flying right elbow and his left foot came off the ground so much in the backswing that just his toes remained in contact with the turf. Lee Trevino rerouted the club—he swung it outside in the backswing and dropped it inside in the downswing. Nick Price has such a quick tempo that if you look away for just a couple of seconds, you miss his entire shot. David Duval plays with a shut face and spins his hips through impact. Jim Furyk has a double-overlap grip, which is the least of his unorthodox moves.

There are also many examples of players who have tried to change the swings that brought them success. After winning three majors in three years—the 1937 and 1938 U.S. Opens and the 1939 Masters—Ralph Guldahl watched his game completely fall apart after he wrote an instructional book called *Groove Your Golf.*

It was a "flip book," consisting of pictures of Guldahl's swing, and unfortunately Guldahl studied those photos and decided he needed to make some changes to his homegrown technique, which had been working just fine.

"He had a peculiar way of playing," fellow competitor Byron Nelson once recalled. "It looked like he was kind of throwing himself at the ball. But he knew what he was doing and could do what he was doing. We didn't take lessons in those days. No doubt if a man learned how to play like he did, and then all of a sudden thought a lot about it, then he was going to get messed up."

Guldahl never won again. The same calamity befell Ian Baker-Finch after he won the 1991 British Open at Royal Birkdale Golf Club in England. Although he was a relatively short hitter, Baker-Finch was one of the best putters in the game. But he decided he could win more if he gained some distance off the tee.

So he tinkered with his swing. Ultimately, he traded in a dependable swing that hit the ball short for a swing that hit the ball longer but couldn't be trusted. While Baker-Finch's swing was fine on the range, he couldn't rely on it on the first tee, leading to some spectacularly off-line shots.

Just four years after his breakthrough win at the 1991 British Open, Baker-Finch had one of his lowest moments during the 1995 British Open, held in St. Andrews, Scotland. At the Old Course, the first and eighteenth holes share a fairway. It is one of the biggest landing areas in golf, measuring 130 yards wide. But somehow, Baker-Finch hooked his drive out of bounds.

Unfortunately, millions of people saw the shot because his playing partner that day was Arnold Palmer, who was playing his final British Open. Two years later, after shooting 92 in the first round of the 1997 British Open at Royal Troon Golf Club, Baker-Finch withdrew and retired from competition.

If either of these champions had gone to Dr. Suttie for help, he no doubt would have recommended that they continue to use the reliable swings that matched their physical tendencies.

Doc shared much of his knowledge in *The LAWs of the Golf Swing*, which he cowrote with Mike Adams and T. J. Tomasi, another instructor. I was one of the first to buy it and loved reading it. I still refer to it often.

The "LAW" in the book's title refers to the three types of swings that golfers use: Leverage, Arc, and Width. The Leverage swing is for players with average build and flexibility—players such as David Toms and Annika Sorenstam. The Arc swing is for tall, flexible players such as Vijay Singh and Michelle Wie, while the Width swing is for players with thicker torsos and less flexibility, such as Craig Stadler.

In the book, Suttie helps readers identify the swing that fits them best, then helps them groove that swing with lessons and drills. But Suttie himself is quick to point out that these three swing types are only a starting point. There are actually few pure Leverage, Arc, or Width swings. Most players have body types that are variations or blends of these three, and it takes a practiced eye like Suttie's to determine the swings that will work for them.

Although the concepts were difficult, Doc somehow explained them in simplified terms that made plenty of sense. Working with Doc has shown me the value of looking beneath the surface, and he has encouraged me to do plenty of research before giving a diagnosis to a student.

MARK'S LESSONS

The great part of golf is that anyone can play it reasonably well. You don't need to be tall and quick like a basketball player, well built or fast like a football player, or possess world-class hand-eye coordination like a baseball player.

However, you do need to adopt the best techniques for your body type. Jim Suttie taught me the importance of looking at both the obvious traits, such as physical build, and the more subtle clues, such as swing tendencies, before making a diagnosis and prescribing a fix.

When you're thinking about making changes to your swing, remember that regardless of your build or swing shape, there is a way for you to play better. Just be careful how you go about improving your game.

HIGH HANDICAPPER

Nobody uses video more effectively than Doc, but he does so selectively. One of his most useful strategies is to videotape his student's swing and then compare it to a tour pro's motion. But he is careful to use a tour pro with a similar height and build. That way, there is an immediate visual connection that the student is more apt to remember.

Even without sophisticated teaching software, this comparison can benefit every golfer. There is plenty you can learn by watching tour pros, whether in person at a tournament, on television, or in the swing sequences that magazines publish every month.

But when you look at the magazines, ignore the sequences of players who don't look like you, and pay particular attention to the players who share your build, especially in the positions that are giving you trouble. If you're taking the club too far to the inside, look at the down-the-line view of the player during the backswing, then try to emulate that position to fix your downswing.

There is no substitute for watching tour pros hitting balls in person. If you do go to a tournament with the aim of learning something, I suggest spending most of your day at the practice range. I used to be based at the TPC Woodlands, then the home of the Shell Houston Open. During the practice days, I would camp out at the practice tee.

While watching for positions is important, pay particular attention to the players' rhythm. Regardless of their build or technique, all tour players have a smooth, effortless swing. But look especially for those who are built like you. You'll instantly relate to their challenges and how they've solved them.

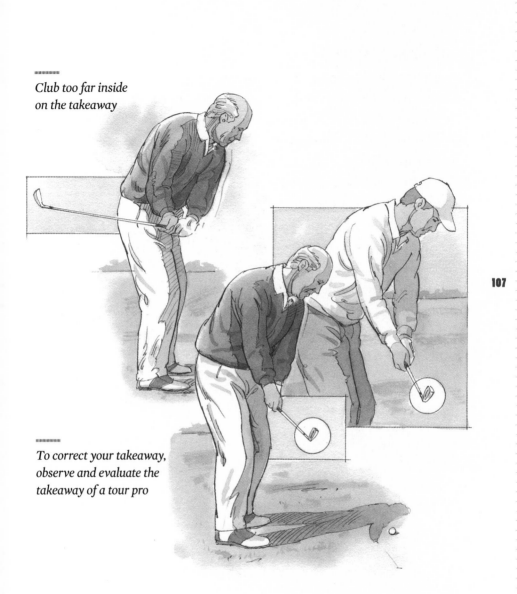

*Club too far inside
on the takeaway*

*To correct your takeaway,
observe and evaluate the
takeaway of a tour pro*

MID HANDICAPPER

As your handicap goes down, you'll find certain patterns emerging in your game. You'll be a low-ball or a high-ball hitter, a drawer or a fader, a hitter or a swinger. These qualities define who you are as a golfer, and it may be difficult to change the DNA of your swing. You'll improve, but within this basic framework.

If you think every tour pro hits towering draws, think again. Jack Nicklaus hit high fades. At his best, Colin Montgomerie played low fades. Billy Casper hooked every shot, even wedges. So did Bobby Locke.

There is no single way to play the game, so also be wary about the next "swing of the month." Over the years, we've seen fads such as Square-to-Square, Connection, Natural Golf, the X-Factor, and most recently, Stack and Tilt.

They may be tempting, but no method is universal. Stack and Tilt, for example, requires quick, flexible hips. Many people don't have that physical ability, so the swing doesn't work for them.

Make changes judiciously, working with your instructor and within the parameters of your body type and swing traits—"matching swing elements," as Doc would call it.

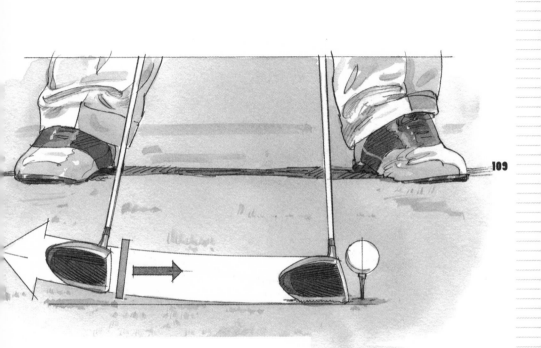

Square-to-Square

The clubface stays square and faces the ball on the takeaway and throughout the swing

Connection
The towel drill fosters the arms staying "connected" to the torso throughout the swing

Natural Golf

The wide stance encourages a level swing down the target line through impact

The X-Factor

The greater the difference between the rotation of the hips and of the shoulders, the more powerful the swing

Stack and Tilt

Rotation points are "stacked" over the left leg

113

LOW HANDICAPPER

Think back to the last time you were "in the zone." What were you thinking about during the swing? If you're like most people, the answer is: Nothing. You simply focused on the target, made the swing, and the ball almost magically landed at the target.

That happens because you have grooved your swing to the point where it is automatic. That is the ultimate goal of golf. Unfortunately, it is rare for all the stars to align so you can reach that point.

More often than not, you'll be fighting your swing to a draw. It may seem like tour pros are always in command of their swings, but they're really in the groove only a few weeks a year. If you examine the tournament results of most players, you'll see that if they play thirty tournaments annually, they make most of their money by finishing in the top ten in only four or five of them. The rest of the time, they either miss the cut or finish in the middle of the pack.

But even when you're not in the zone, you can help groove your swing by developing feel-oriented swing thoughts that will either promote the action you desire or prevent the fault that you most want to avoid. For example, Joel Edwards's tendency has been to approach impact from too far inside the target line, which means he has to flip the club through impact, often resulting in low hooks. For a short hitter who needed as much carry distance as possible, this error could be disastrous.

So he made numerous practice swings with an over-the-top, out-to-in move from the top. This swing preparation is the last thing the average player needs, but for Edwards, it was the remedy for matching his tendencies.

Like Edwards, you can play your best golf when you are familiar with your tendencies and groove a swing so that you can be in the zone more often. Help this process along by making sure that you are mentally prepared to hit the ball following your pre-shot routine. If you feel even the slightest twinge of doubt or discomfort, start your routine again. An unsettled mind will cause off-line shots.

PAUL MARCHAND

Fred Couples's fluid motion is the result of his work with
Paul Marchand, who in my opinion, is one of the most un-
derrated teachers in the game.

Paul knows swing mechanics, but he is a big believer
in good rhythm, which can make up for plenty of faults
during the swing. When I have students who have a solid
swing but are going through slumps, I usually have them
focus on tempo.

Paul's lesson is also applicable for a common mid round
malady; every golfer has inexplicably lost control of his or her
swing induring a round. The next time that happens, don't
worry about the position of your hands or the length of your
backswing. Instead, try to make your swing as fluid as that of
Fred Couples. That should help you come out of your slump.

HARVEY PENICK
Golf's First Psychologist

There has never been a better swing thought in golf than "Take dead aim." In fact, those three words make up what is the most memorable lesson from *Harvey Penick's Little Red Book*.

I heard Harvey give this advice to many students, and I myself have used it often while playing. I found it most useful in uncomfortable situations: during tournaments and periods in which I was making changes to my swing. In those cases, the tendency is to focus too much on swing mechanics or the scorecard: Where is my ball position? Is my swing too upright? Do I need to make a birdie on this hole?

Any experienced golfer can tell you that overthinking is the quickest way to have your round go downhill. Golfers play their best when they are in the zone, a state in which they play with seemingly no thoughts at all.

The beauty of "Take dead aim" is that it eliminates all thoughts except the target itself, which, when you think about it, should be exactly what you're focusing on anyway. After all, golf is a target-based game, whether your target is the flagstick, a portion of the fairway, or the hole itself.

When the stakes are big enough, even tour pros have trouble with short putts. At the 2001 U.S. Open at Southern Hills Country Club in Tulsa, Oklahoma, Retief Goosen had a one-shot lead as he teed off on the difficult par-four finishing hole. All he needed was a par to win. After a good drive, Goosen hit a great iron to twelve feet, seemingly all but wrapping up his first major championship. After all, a tour pro like Goosen could probably two-putt from twelve feet with his eyes closed.

He hit his first putt well, and it nearly went in. The ball finished less than two feet past the hole, a virtual tap-in. In a casual match or in a match-play event, an opponent would have conceded Goosen a putt of that distance.

But Goosen missed the putt to make bogey and fell into a tie with Mark Brooks. Fortunately, he won the eighteen-hole playoff the next day to win the first of his two U.S. Open titles.

But Goosen might have won a day earlier had he focused on the target and just tapped the ball into the hole. This positive thought would have kept Goosen from dwelling on the negatives, such as the consequences of a missed putt.

The best example of a player with positive focus is Tiger Woods, the most mentally strong player I have ever watched play the game. Dating back to his junior days, Woods has made the putts he had to make on the last couple of holes, especially in the biggest events.

Woods owes much of his mental toughness to his late father, Earl, a former Green Beret. Earl was a good player, but he left the swing instruction of his son to qualified teachers. Instead, Earl subjected young Tiger to a rash of games-manship so that he would not be rattled by any situation on the course.

Besides standing over short, must-make putts, golfers most often fall into negative states of mind when they are in scoring zones they have never experienced before, whether it's a chance to break 100 for the first time or coming down the stretch with a chance to win the club championship.

Earl Woods did something brilliant to ensure that his son never felt anxious about going low. When Tiger was young, Earl assigned him a "personal par" for each hole. On a long-par hole, that personal par might be eight. If Tiger made a seven, it would be a birdie. At the end of the nine holes, Tiger might be three or four shots below his personal par.

An average person might choke at the chance to be three under par for nine holes, but that was normal for Tiger. As Tiger got better, Earl gradually lowered his personal par. But as long he kept his scores below his personal par, no scoring barrier would scare him.

Because his father instilled success into his game from the start, there seems to be little negativity in Woods's thought process. That's an approach that Harvey would have endorsed wholeheartedly. When giving lessons or advice, Harvey refrained from using negative words such as "never" and "don't."

Once, Tom Kite came to him for some help with putting. Harvey asked him what had changed since their last lesson. Kite said that he had started choking down on the putter.

Harvey's reply was adamant. "Tommy, don't use that word," he said. "You should never use the word 'choke' in connection with your golf game. Don't think of choking down on your putter—think of gripping down on it."

Kite considered that response to be psychology, and I do too. In fact, I believe that Harvey's approach to teaching the game made him the first golf psychologist. Nowadays, nearly every top player employs a sports psychologist to help him or her prepare mentally for each round and each shot.

In addition to fixing their slices or helping them with their bunker shots, Harvey made sure his students were confident when they stepped to the first tee. He helped them to see the game in a different way, so they were prepared mentally for each shot and made the best swing possible. This psychology probably helped his students more than the swing tips ever did, because while the physical side can come and go from day to day, the mental side can always be in top form.

Other players can match Tiger Woods's best shots. The key to his success is that Woods's bad shots are better than the bad shots of the other players. Physical skill and talent have something to do with that, but not as much as mental preparedness. Many bad shots are the result of indecision or letting the mind wander, and that rarely happens to Woods. A strong mind can overcome plenty of physical faults.

Once, a man came from New York to Austin for a lesson with Harvey, and said, "If you're such a great teacher, teach me how to get out of sand traps."

Replied Harvey: "Not so fast. I can teach you how to get out of sand traps. But I'm not going to do it until I teach you how to avoid getting into them in the first place."

I'm sure the student felt more comfortable with his entire game—not just sand play—after the lesson. That was the effect that Harvey the psychologist had on people. He knew that he could help someone with a specific fault, but it was more effective to help the student feel more confident and focused on *every* shot.

Harvey used trick shots sometimes in his teaching, and one of his favorites was making a full swing with a wedge so the ball flew straight up in the air and he could catch it.

I once asked him how to do it. Instead of telling me, he suggested I figure it out for myself. Needless to say, I was at the range practicing for a long time. But I did figure it out, and in the process, I improved my hand-eye coordination and developed a better understanding of the relationship between the club and the ball, which I could use in my own teaching.

Harvey knew that it was important for me to do this on my own, which is why he provided minimal instruction. He knew what I needed and guided me toward that discovery. That is what a psychologist does.

Harvey always made his students feel comfortable—another bit of psychology. I know from experience that it is difficult to help students who are so nervous that they don't hit their normal shots. And if they can't show you how they play in a more familiar, relaxed situation, you can't figure out what you should be helping them to improve.

Harvey had a solution. He began each lesson with a chat, especially if the students were first-timers. He would want to know about the problems in their games and how long they had been off. Besides putting his students at ease, he would shift the burden of improvement from the pupil to himself. "Any mistakes that are made out there today are mine, not yours," he would say. And that usually worked. It's a technique I try to use during my own lessons with students.

But no matter who his students were, Harvey invariably got them to trust in their own basic abilities, their swings—and take dead aim.

MARK'S LESSONS

Taking dead aim is a perfect swing thought. It focuses your mind and keeps your thoughts positive, blocking out the tension and negativity that can build up, especially on stressful situations or the first tee shot. But the question remains: Exactly where should you take dead aim? The answer depends on your skill level.

HIGH HANDICAPPER

No matter what club you have in your hand, aim for the widest, most hazard-free area you can find. On a hole with woods or water down the right side, line up on the extreme right side of the tee box and aim down the left side. And keep in mind that high handicappers tend to miss shots short of the target, instead of to the left or right.

If the entire front of the green is well guarded, it may make more sense to lay up with a wedge. But that strategy doesn't work if you miss your lay-up target. So even when you're laying up, pick a target that gives you plenty of room for error. Players tend to make their best, most carefree swings when there are no obstacles to avoid, so try to make that happen whenever possible.

MID HANDICAPPER

By now, your shots have a distinct pattern, so keep that in mind when you're aiming and take advantage of your shot shape.

Let's say your natural ball flight is a fade and you're on the tee of a narrow hole with a fairway that is thirty yards wide. If you aim down the middle, your ball has to fade no more than fifteen yards to stay in the fairway. However, if you aim down the left edge of the fairway, the ball can fade up to thirty yards and still hit the short grass for your next shot. In short, you've just doubled the size of your landing area. I like those odds.

LOW HANDICAPPER

Taking dead aim is most applicable when you're firing at the flagstick. I agree that there is no feeling more satisfying in golf than watching a shot head straight toward the pin. And tapping in for birdie can send you to the next tee with a bounce in your step.

But it's important to realize that firing at pins near water hazards or tucked behind bunkers is not a good strategy. Just a slight miss can land you in trouble, resulting in bogey or worse. These dangerous hole locations aren't known as "sucker pins" for nothing.

If you play in tournaments, the committee usually sets up the course with six easy hole locations, six medium ones, and six difficult ones. Learn to recognize the different locations and assign a traffic-light color to each. The easy locations are the green lights, so you can aim right at them. For the medium locations, or yellow lights, you can fire at the pin if you're feeling confident, are hitting a short iron, or if the shot fits your natural shot shape. In other words, go ahead, but use common sense.

For the hard locations, or the red lights, stay away at all costs. Aim for the middle of the green to avoid being suckered into making a big number. You can still take dead aim—just at the biggest part of the green.

CHARLIE EPPS

I spent a lot of time with Charlie Epps while we were working for the Nicklaus/Flick Golf Schools. His greatest strength is making the game more enjoyable for his students. Charlie helped Angel Cabrera win the 2009 Masters by keeping the intense Argentine star relaxed between and during the pressure-filled rounds.

For Charlie, hitting buckets of range balls can begin to feel like work. You can make improvement fun by practicing imaginative shots, the same way Cabrera hits practice shots out of the trees under Charlie's guidance. By hitting shots left, right, low, and high, you'll develop control over the ball, which will help you hit better shots from any position on the course.

KATHY WHITWORTH

The Super Lady Project

Here's a trivia question: **Who has won the most tournaments in** professional golf?

It's not Tiger Woods, who had won sixty-eight tournaments by mid-2009. It's not Jack Nicklaus. With seventy-three victories, he isn't even tops on the PGA Tour. (That distinction belongs to Sam Snead, who won eighty-two times.) And it's not Annika Sorenstam, who has won seventy-two times.

No, the answer is Kathy Whitworth, the winner of eighty-eight LPGA tournaments, including six major championships. Not a physically talented phenom like Nicklaus or Woods, Kathy achieved her success through determination and hard work.

In fact, when she first came on the LPGA Tour in 1959, absolutely nobody—including Kathy herself—would have imagined that she would be the winningest professional golfer in history. That year, her scoring average was more than 80, and she made just twelve hundred dollars the entire season. She didn't earn her first check until the thirteenth tournament of the season. (Coincidentally, that week she earned thirty dollars, roughly the same amount as Nicklaus's first check three years later.)

She had occasional thoughts about giving up, but she willed herself not only to make it on the tour but also to become one of its standard-bearers. In that regard, Whitworth is the female equivalent of Ben Hogan, who also struggled early in his career before "digging it out of the dirt" to become one of golf's all-time legendary players. So it's no surprise that Kathy now makes her home at the Trophy Club Country Club, once Hogan's refuge.

It was quite an honor when I received a chance to work with the most successful champion in golf history on a unique program known as *The Super Lady Project*.

In 1990 a group from Japan came to Kathy and asked her to teach eight girls—a mixture of beginners and intermediates—with the goal of creating professional golfers who could play on the Japanese LPGA Tour, in two short years. This group thought that the way golf was being taught was all wrong, and wanted the program to show that these girls could learn in a completely different way.

Sho Tobari, a prominent Japanese announcer, enlisted the help of Random Associates, a talent agency, to choose the girls. The selection process was rigorous; the judges were looking for mental toughness, competitiveness, and physical skill.

Thousands of girls from all over Japan applied to be among the eight winners picked to move to the United States for the program. Two of the girls selected had never played golf, but were competitive in softball and swimming.

A precursor to today's reality-television shows like *The Big Break*, *The Super Lady Project* was broadcast throughout Japan. Although the girls were young, they had talents in areas Kathy thought could be cultivated.

Once the girls were chosen, Kathy oversaw their training. Betsy Cullen and I were the swing coaches, while Kathy got the girls ready for competition.

The Japanese sponsors thought traditional teaching methods were insufficient, and they may have been right. The project forced me to overhaul my approach. Until then, I had taught in one-hour blocks, seeing my pupils weekly at most. But because these eight girls would be immersed in the game for two years, there were a lot of questions Kathy, Betsy, and I had to ponder before we started.

How many lessons did they need? Per week? Per month? When should they start playing tournaments? What would be their fitness schedule? How much should they work on the mental side? What would they need in terms of equipment?

When I look back on it, I realize that we were very much ahead of our time, as the teaching industry has since evolved to embrace this type of holistic approach. But at the time, all this was quite new to us. Updates on how the girls were progressing would be shown on Fuji Television, which put pressure on us to produce results.

But the real pressure was on the eight girls. Not only were they young (ranging in age from seventeen to twenty-two), but they also had to leave their homes and live in a foreign country for two years. They all lived together in a nice house, so there were really no breaks from the project. All they did was practice, eat, and sleep.

Early on, the biggest impediment was the language barrier. We had an interpreter, but it was clear that not every lesson was getting through, which probably wasn't a bad thing at first, because Betsy and I were giving them a lot of information.

After a while, the problem was less the language difference and more cultural one. They were so used to following instructions without questioning that it was often unclear whether they even understood what we were saying. They would nod and do whatever we said, regardless of whether it was working. That docility may sound great from a teacher's standpoint, but it actually hurt the students. The lack of feedback meant I had no idea whether the lessons were taking hold.

But as we got to know one another better, the relationships improved. They did start asking questions, and I felt that our sessions were becoming more productive. What never changed was that, despite my insistence that they refer to me as "Mark," they continued to call me "Mr. Steinbauer." In Japanese culture, the teacher is to be treated with respect at all times.

The girls came to us with varying degrees of golf experience. Before the project started, we consulted with Harvey, hoping to get some advice on how best to teach each of them. He said that it would be easy to drown them in mechanical advice and warned us not to overteach them.

He was right, of course. The project proved to be enlightening on a number of levels. First, it was particularly difficult to change their swings, no matter how many lessons we had or how many balls they hit. There aren't many grass ranges in Japan, which meant our girls were used to hitting off rubber mats at urban driving ranges. It was curious to see that this experience caused many of them to develop the same problems: strong grip, shut clubface, and a swing plane that was too vertical. They were truly a product of their environment. This led to the most heated discussion that Kathy, Betsy, and I had.

A stronger grip requires players to rotate more through impact; otherwise they'll hook the ball too much. Kathy was adamant that the girls should have a neutral grip (with the right hand more on top of the club rather than underneath) and swing into a "firm" left side, which meant that they should face the ball at impact rather than rotating out of the way.

The message from Kathy was loud and clear: "If you can't grip the club correctly, you can't play." Jack Nicklaus also swung into a firm left side, and he and Kathy were two of the greatest players in history.

Still, no matter how much Betsy and I tried to get the girls to change their grips, the results were less than satisfactory. Their hands were small, and they had a tough time with gripping the club the way Kathy instructed. After a while, we realized that our "one-size-fits-all" philosophy wasn't working. We had eight different girls with eight different swings, gifts, and talents, and our classroom approach had to go.

That led me to think about how junior golfers develop in the United States. Until recently, most kids started playing with cut-down adult clubs that were still both too long and too heavy for them. So instead of swinging the club correctly in the backswing, they had to find a way to lift the club to the top.

That is what produced Nancy Lopez's unique backswing set-up. And if you look at photographs of Justin Leonard at age eight, he is standing erect with a club that is too long for him. Nearly thirty years later, his setup hasn't changed much.

My point is that kids form their swings early in their golf lives, and it is difficult to change much. I have seen only two players who have altered their swings noticeably: Tom Kite and Nick Faldo. And they are two of the hardest workers in the history of the game.

The second lesson I learned from these eight girls was that there was more than one way to swing a club. Each girl in the project swung the club slightly differently, and before I could help them, I had to familiarize myself with their individual strengths and weaknesses. I really had to study them, both on the driving range and on the course. I don't know how top instructors teach ten to twenty tour players and do a thorough job with each of them. I have to applaud their ability to juggle that many players.

Eventually, I became less of a teacher and more of a coach to these girls. We spent less time changing swings and more time on the course, learning how to play—how to handle different situations and get the ball in the hole quicker.

After all, the goal was to help them succeed in tournaments. And what was surprising to me was how well they did in competition.

Most players take a while to learn to play as well in tournaments as they do in casual play. They aren't playing with friends who make them feel comfortable, and they can't take mulligans off the first tee if they hit bad drives. And instead of taking a gimme after lagging an approach putt to two feet, they have to putt everything out.

Believe me, when every shot counts, a two-foot putt is no given. Even tour pros have been known to miss gimmes. It takes a while to get into the mind-set of performing under this kind of pressure, whether you're playing the club championship, a local amateur tournament, or the Masters. But to my surprise, I found that most of the Japanese girls actually played better when every shot counted. Most of them had played other sports and were used to the pressure. They came to the project with strong mental games already, so that wasn't something that we needed to work on much.

In Japan there was tremendous interest in how the girls were progressing. One of the best players was the youngest, Shoko Asano. She was seventeen and progressed quite quickly, qualifying for the U.S. Women's Open in 1992.

Cameras followed her everywhere that week at Oakmont Country Club in Oakmont, Pennsylvania, and her shirt had so many logos that she looked like a NASCAR driver. While she played, there were fifty members of the Japanese press following her every step. I doubt any golfer except Tiger Woods has endured that much media attention at a tournament.

Although she missed the cut, I thought that if for her alone, *The Super Lady Project* was successful. It was remarkable that in a year, a beginning golfer became good enough to play in the U.S. Women's Open.

But back in Japan, the standards were much higher, so the outcome was mixed in their eyes. Sure, it was nice that several of the girls wound up later playing on the Japanese LPGA Tour. But I think they were hoping to produce another Kathy Whitworth. The sponsors wanted the girls to become stars so that they could sign them to long-term contracts.

Perhaps if we could have worked with the girls for longer, one of them might have become a top player. The concept of intensive instruction has worked in the past. Similar training camps are exactly what produced world-class golfers from countries such as Sweden and Australia.

One of the biggest downsides of full-immersion programs is that their participants can become one-dimensional. While the girls' first, second, and third priorities were to play golf, I noticed that they needed time away from the game and one another. When they took a break and made some trips to places such as the Johnson Space Center, the Galleria, and the beach, they played better when they returned.

I have found that tour players need similar breaks. If they play in too many events in a row, they get mentally exhausted. They can't focus as well and start making mistakes. They need a couple of weeks away from the tour to regroup.

Kathy knew that better than anyone; but when it came to our project, she expected a lot of the girls, who toiled at perfecting their craft and were certainly able to match Kathy's work ethic and intensity.

I am thankful to have been involved in such a unique project, and the experience helped me to bring a holistic approach to my lessons ever since.

MARK'S LESSONS

Nobody doubts that golf is a difficult game, and every pro has gone through stretches that have tested his or her will. The best players overcome these challenges and emerge as better golfers.

But the key is to remain positive and not get too discouraged in the face of disappointments, challenges, and far-off goals. If you're in a slump, identify the problem and find a way to get through it. Honing your inner determination will help you become a better golfer under all conditions.

HIGH HANDICAPPER

Beginning players are sponges for information. The problem is that they often get too much advice from too many sources, and their knowledge base isn't sophisticated enough to filter the good from the bad.

This can be confusing at best, harmful at worst. I know that it's tempting to try every tip that you read or hear, but it makes more sense to find a teacher you trust and work with that teacher to navigate through golf's difficulties. You'll develop a better understanding of your own game, and you'll be a better player in the long run.

MID HANDICAPPER

We've all had days when we just don't have it. Your setup is uncomfortable and your swing feels foreign. Warming up, you may find that the fade you normally hit is a slice.

We've also had days in which the wheels have come off in the middle of a round. Even on the PGA Tour, few players are dialed in for all four rounds—even the winners. Instead, they are able to shoot a decent score with a good short game, which is the lesson you should learn.

You're going to miss a lot of greens on off days, so practice distance control with your wedge. On the range, learn what pitches of thirty, forty, fifty, and sixty yards feel like. Start with a thirty-yard shot, then move up in ten-yard increments. Most likely, you'll control the distance with the length of the backswing—the longer the shot, the longer the backswing.

A reliable pitching motion will change the way you play during a swing slump. When you miss a fairway, you'll be confident in laying up to about forty or fifty yards short of the hole, knowing that you'll have a chance to make par. This skill will save a lot of bad rounds—and frustration.

LOW HANDICAPPER

For many good players, the key to weathering slumps is in their minds, not their swings. You have to develop mental toughness, and there is no better way to do that than to play with golfers who are better than you.

Seek out your club champion or your pro and play as often as possible with that person. Early in the week at tour events, Blaine McCallister would play money matches against tough competitors like Ray Floyd. Blaine wanted to see how long he could "stay in the ring" with better players.

You may find that these better players don't necessarily have better swings. You can hit any shot that they can. In other words, your highs are just as high as theirs. The difference is that their lows are much higher than your lows because they are more focused and make fewer mistakes.

Keep arranging these matches, and you'll become more competitive.

ROGER CLEVELAND

At the Callaway Test Center, noted club designer Roger Cleveland showed me how the sole of a wedge moves through the grass or the sand, and how the angle between the sole and the club's leading edge, known as the bounce, affects the shot. He also showed me how changing the bounce could help personalize a wedge to fit each golfer's needs.

You don't need to have decades of experience designing clubs to pick the right wedge. If you have a shallow swing path (you pick the ball off the grass with your irons) or play courses with tightly mown turf, use a wedge with less bounce (4–8°). If you have a steep path (you take big divots) or play lush courses, try a wedge with more bounce (10–14°).

JIM FLICK

Swing, Don't Hit

Golf instruction has evolved considerably since I got started in the business more than twenty-five years ago. The equipment available now to golf teachers is far more sophisticated. Advancements such as portable video cameras, computers, and launch monitors have allowed us to study the swing as never before.

Golf cable networks and Web sites have offered new avenues for teachers to disseminate information to the masses. And this exposure, along with the emergence of so-called tour gurus, has made celebrities of many instructors.

Truth is, while they may be more rich and famous now, top teachers have always been well known in the industry; and other instructors have sought them out to learn from their expertise. For decades, many teachers shared their knowledge by working together in golf schools.

Not only did golf schools allow students to learn from several top teachers at once, they also allowed the instructors to trade ideas and learn from one another in a nonclassroom setting. Sadly, another change in the golf instruction industry has been a dramatic decrease in the popularity of golf schools, giving instructors fewer opportunities to work together.

If not for golf schools, I never would have had a chance to learn from Jim Flick, who began working with the Golf Digest Schools in 1972 and became the schools' director of instruction in 1976.

The staff of the Golf Digest Schools was a Hall of Fame lineup: In addition to Flick, it featured Paul Runyan, Davis Love Jr., Bob Toski, and Jack Lumpkin. And as if that weren't enough, Sam Snead was a frequent guest instructor. What I would have given to be a fly on the wall when that group went out to dinner.

Hanging out with big names was nothing new for Jim. In college at Wake Forest, one of his roommates and teammates had been Arnold Palmer. Then at the 1990 Tradition, Jim ran into Jack Nicklaus, who was headed out to play a practice round before his first tournament on the Senior PGA Tour. Jim asked to follow along.

The year before, Nicklaus's longtime teacher, Jack Grout, had passed away. Grout had been Nicklaus's instructor since he was ten, so Nicklaus was feeling directionless that day at Desert Mountain. Naturally, he asked Flick for some advice as the pair walked up the eighteenth fairway.

"What I don't see is Jack Nicklaus," Flick said. At the range afterward, Flick told Nicklaus that the feel was missing from his swing, and he helped him regain it. It worked, as Nicklaus won his first Senior Tour.

The pair worked so well together, in fact, that they went into business as a team, forming the Nicklaus/Flick Golf Schools the following year. Jim hired a number of instructors from the Golf Digest Schools, all of whom he knew wouldn't need much training. One of them, a Houston-based instructor named Charlie Epps convinced Jim to hire me. I left the Academy of Golf, excited about not only the chance to work with Jim, but also being exposed to a different teaching philosophy.

At the Academy, largely due to Bill Moretti's association with David Leadbetter, we had mostly taught swing techniques that focused on the big muscles of the legs, hips, and torso. Jim taught the opposite: One of the main tenets of his teaching was emphasis on the swinging action of the motion controlled by the hands, wrists, and arms.

Whenever Jim gave a clinic or presentation at the beginning of a school, he would invariably ask leading questions in order to get a student to ask whether power could be generated without focusing on the turning of big muscles. That was Jim's cue to perform his favorite demonstration: hitting a driver while kneeling.

In this position, he could barely rotate his torso. With just his arms, Jim would hit a drive of more than two hundred yards every time, to the delight of his students. If he didn't have everyone's attention before, he had it now. After that, the whole class was eager to hear Jim's advice and instruction.

Demonstrating his points was what Jim did best. And his passion for the subject was so strong that he could sit with one student for hours, offering guidance until his or her swing finally clicked. Even in a school of a dozen students, Jim made each one feel like he or she was receiving a private lesson.

From Jim, I learned the importance of earning a student's trust. Jim had such a strong bond with his students that he could tell them to swing the club one-handed and they would do so.

One part of the Nicklaus/Flick philosophy that was an eye-opener for me was the way we taught the same principles in both the full swing and the short game. At most golf schools, we divided the class into two groups. One group worked on the full swing while the other focused on the short game. But we never coordinated the methods of the two groups until I got to the Nicklaus/Flick Schools.

My responsibility at most of the schools was the short game. Although I wasn't familiar with Flick's method until I started working for him, I had to immerse myself in it in order to send a message that was compatible with the full-swing approach, which was a swing of the arms with a slight inside loop in the downswing.

It's not so easy to play short shots, especially bunker shots, with an inside loop. A slight out-to-in path is actually best for the short game. But my mandate was to teach the short game to students with this swing shape, and I figured out a way to make it work. It wasn't easy, but that was what made success that much more rewarding.

Not every instructor would have been able to teach this method. But Flick devised an effective orientation program and hired a talented group of teachers. If the staff of the Golf Digest Schools was made up of Hall of Famers, the Nicklaus/Flick Schools boasted an all-star lineup.

My roommate during the training program was Martin Hall, an Englishman responsible for some of the most innovative ideas in the business. Martin has had plenty of success teaching female players, including his wife, Lisa, and Morgan Pressel, who at the age of eighteen became the youngest major winner in LPGA Tour history.

Other teachers recruited by Flick included Dean Reinmuth, who was Phil Mickelson's longtime instructor; Laird Small, who has built a successful teaching program at Pebble Beach; Mike Malaska, who became one of the leading proponents of combining instruction with physical fitness; and Mark Wood, who has taught many tour pros, including Dudley Hart. All went on to be named by the golf magazines as the best instructors in the country.

We all came into the schools with different backgrounds and had some interesting conversations with Jim, both one-on-one and in a group setting. Although Jim liked to teach a certain method, he knew that there were other schools of thought out there. He invited discussion and even arguments, but he often challenged your points of view and made you back them up with facts or examples.

What I took away from my time with Jim was the way he was able to simplify a complicated game by encouraging his students to develop feel during the motion and to swing the club with the arms instead of relying on the torso and legs.

Now when a student tries to overcomplicate the swing, I take a cue from Jim and hit the ball off my knees to demonstrate how easy the game can be. It works every time.

MARK'S LESSONS

Jim Flick is a big proponent of being aware of what the club is doing during the swing. Since the hands are the only parts of the body connected to the club, he focuses on enhancing feel in the small muscles of the hands and arms.

Thinking about feel helps avoid the paralysis that results from having mechanical thoughts during the swing. It helps you to swing the club freely so you can build clubhead speed and square up the club at impact for longer, straighter shots. Here are some drills for enhancing feel.

HIGH HANDICAPPER

Jim's demonstration of hitting balls from his knees is actually a great way to learn to swing freely and close the clubhead through impact. Make sure to use a driver and tee the ball high. I wouldn't recommend performing this drill with any other club. Put a towel under your knees for comfort, and set up far enough away from the ball so that your arms are extended. This position promotes a flat swing plane, like that of a baseball swing.

Since your body is fixed in place, you will be able to swing freely and the clubhead will close naturally without any manipulation. Observe this closing action and try to re-create it when you're back on your feet.

A less extreme variation of this drill is to hit balls with your feet together. Use a mid or short iron and tee up the ball. Not only does this drill ingrain the feel of swinging the club, it will quickly identify whether you have good balance. If you don't, you'll fall over.

MID HANDICAPPER

Jim always stressed the importance of being aware of the club's position during the swing. He liked to prescribe an exercise to build feel for the clubhead.

Take an iron with your normal grip, then hold it in front of you with your hands at belt height. Close your eyes, then twirl the club in your hands before tightening the grip. With your eyes still closed, try to guess the direction in which the clubhead is pointing—up, down, to the side—by gauging the weight distribution. (Don't use a club that has a grip with a reminder bar down the bottom; that's cheating.)

You can only guess accurately with a light hold on the club. And it will take some practice before your hands and arms become sensitive enough to get it right. But once you do, you'll find that your feel for the club, as well as your control over it, improves greatly.

147

JIM FLICK: SWING, DON'T HIT

LOW HANDICAPPER

One unique aspect of Jim's schools was their emphasis on playing. In addition to sessions on the long game and the short game, he wanted his students to undergo at least one on-course lesson.

For most good players, the part of the swing that starts to unravel on the course is not mechanics but rhythm and timing, especially in the transition between the backswing and downswing.

Develop rhythm with Jim's step-in drill. With an iron and a ball on tee, set up normally at address. Then move the left foot (for right-handers) away from the target so it is next to the right foot. Take the club back, but before the club reaches the top of the backswing, step toward the target with the left foot, the way a baseball player at bat strides toward the pitcher.

This will ensure that the downswing starts properly, from the feet up, and the arms and club will drop correctly into the proper position to hit the ball solidly and along the correct path. Jerking the club down with the shoulders and arms throws off the swing's timing

The step-in is also a good way to make practice swings to ingrain the feel of the proper rhythm and timing that you need to straighten out your game.

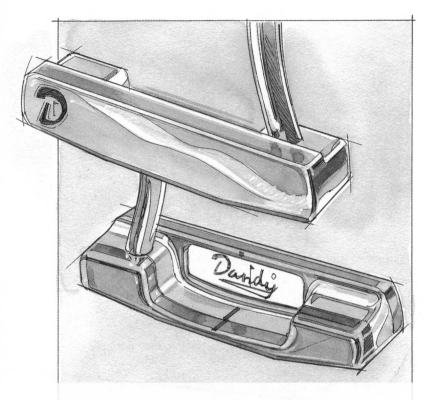

DANDY PUTTERS

More Than One Way to Get the Ball in the Hole

Whether you're a high handicapper or a professional golfer, putting is an extremely important part of the game. For somebody trying to break 90 for the first time, it may be possible to do so by avoiding a three-putt green for the entire round. At a PGA Tour event, a few missed putts could be the difference between missing the cut and being in contention for the weekend.

Although improved putting is the quickest way to lower scores, it is the most fickle part of the game. A swing change like fixing an overly strong grip can have a big effect right away in the full swing, but there are no similarly obvious Band-Aids in putting.

Sure, there are some fundamentals that really help. The eyes should be directly over the ball or just behind it on the target line. The putter face must be square, and impact must occur on the sweet spot for consistent results.

(The alignment aid on the top of most putters indicates the sweet spot. To be sure where it is, hold the putter halfway up the shaft so it dangles and swings freely. Tap the putter face with the sharp end of a tee until you find the point where you cause the putter to swing straight back, with the heel and toe moving evenly.)

Other than that, pretty much anything goes. Ben Crenshaw stands mostly upright and lets his arms hang straight. For a while, Jack Nicklaus had success putting with a stance that was so bent over that his right forearm was parallel to the ground. Arnold Palmer crouched over the putt so much that he looked as if he were trying to open a jar of pickles. His feet were pigeon-toed and his knees were together, and he rapped the putt with a wristy stroke. Bobby Locke hooked every putt, making contact with a stroke that brought the putter head into the ball from extremely inside the target line.

It isn't just the setup and stroke that varies. So does the length of the shaft. For a while, some players tried the "belly putter," a mid-length club used with the butt end resting against the stomach during the stroke, stabilizing the club and the head for better impact. Many senior players, including Orville Moody, had more success after switching to a long putter.

Bernhard Langer, who experimented with a number of different techniques, including running his left arm down the shaft of the putter and grasping both the left arm and putter grip with his right hand, suffered from the yips (an unwelcome, jerky stroke on short putts) throughout his career and has found innovative ways of overcoming them, most notably with the long putter. Langer also tried putting cross-handed or "left-hand low," a grip that has become so universally accepted that nobody even points it out anymore; though when players first started using the grip, it was seen as a curiosity.

Other grips that have brought success to players include "the claw," in which the player turns his right hand over and grips the club with the palm facing down, so the stroke is made primarily with the right hand.

All these techniques demonstrate that there is no single way to putt well. More important, they show that no matter how poorly you putt, there is hope. Unlike the full swing, you don't need as much athletic ability, timing, flexibility, and strength to putt like a tour pro. All you need is the right fundamentals, a good mental approach, and the right piece of equipment.

Don't underestimate the importance of having the right putter for your stroke. It makes a huge difference. Nowadays, with high-speed cameras and advanced fitting systems, it is possible to see exactly how the ball comes off the putter head. The goal is to have the ball rolling as soon as possible after impact. Any bouncing will cause the ball to stop short of the target.

But a properly struck putt will roll out, providing feedback for how hard to hit the next putt—a key for distance control, which is the most important aspect of putting. In addition, a true-rolling ball is less susceptible to being knocked off line by small imperfections on the putting surface. The high-speed cameras show that changing the putter has an effect on the ball's roll. So the key is to find a putter that fits your stroke.

I am simplifying matters a bit, but there are basically two different ways to putt. In the first method, the putter head stays on the target line—in the backstroke, through impact, and into the follow-through—for as long as possible, while the putter face remains square, or perpendicular, to that line.

This stroke seeks to simplify putting by reducing the act to a single, pendulum-like action. Noted short-game teacher Dave Pelz is the biggest proponent of the pendulum stroke.

In the second approach, the putter head moves to the inside of the target line in the backstroke, returns to the target line through impact, and moves back inside the target line after impact. This inside-square-inside move requires players to close the putter face through impact like a door on a hinge. This action has gained popularity on tour, thanks largely to its most successful practitioner, Tiger Woods.

When teaching putting, I used to not worry so much about whether my students' putters matched their different strokes. I used to look at their posture, whether their eyes were over the ball, whether their arms and shoulders were aligned squarely to the target. I'd work on their pre-shot routines and preach the importance of not peeking, which causes the head to move before impact, altering the path of the stroke. And I often prescribed drills to develop feel and consistency.

But now one of the first things I do is check whether my student's putter matches his or her stroke. And that's thanks to the Strand brothers, Everett and Allan.

Like me, they are from Minnesota. In 1995 they formed a putter company, Dandy. In the early years of the company, I offered feedback on the different models they built, commenting on the putter's feel, weight, cosmetics, and performance. Allan and Everett thought that the most popular styles of clubs weren't compatible with what they believed was the best way to putt.

One of the players Everett studied in depth was Horton Smith, the winner of two of the first three Masters. I, too, had studied Smith's putting style, largely because of Harvey Penick, who used to talk about the way Smith arched his wrists in the backstroke to keep the putter on the target, with the shaft leaning forward and the grip much closer to the hole.

Everett's design is the first putter to fit Smith's method. Instead of coming straight up from the putter head like a standard putter, the shaft leans forward, to match the angle of your left arm, and meets the head behind the face, so the golfer can get a clear look at the ball.

Finally, the grip is unique. With a standard putting grip, the top is flat, so players can rest their thumbs on it. In the Dandy, the flat part is rotated counterclockwise so the flat surface faces the target. This allows the left palm to cradle the grip, enhancing the feeling that the putter is an extension of the left arm.

This setup causes the left wrist to arch into the position that Smith favored while putting. From here, there is no way for the back of the left wrist to break down during the stroke. The putter remains square and along the target line throughout the stroke.

I was impressed, and thought that the new design could help a lot of my students. But I never thought that a putter could change a player's putting stroke until I saw Dr. Gil Morgan using a Dandy.

Gil Morgan is an optometrist, but soon after earning his degree he realized that he could make a better living staring down putts than he could examining patients' eyes. Morgan went on to win seven PGA Tour events, but his biggest successes came after he turned fifty in 1996. He has won twenty-five senior events, including three majors. Part of that success was due to the use of a Dandy putter.

I witnessed the transformation on the practice green during an event. Morgan warmed up using a Ping Anser, the popular blade-style putter he had used for much of his career. When viewed from above, his stroke had a lot of arc. He would take the putter well inside the target line in the backstroke, with the face rotating open correspondingly. The stroke resembled the curving action of a windshield wiper.

Morgan then switched to a Dandy, and on the very next putt, he was like a different player. The putter head only moved slightly to the inside going back and after impact. If Dandy had been around during Morgan's prime, I believe Morgan would have won a major with it.

Unfortunately, although the Strands have built a terrific product, it takes more than that to build a well-known brand. The company received a boost with Morgan's play and especially from Vijay Singh, who won the 2000 Masters with a Dandy putter.

However, a lot of other competitors have unique stories like that of Dandy. SeeMore putters have a visual alignment system on the top of the putter head consisting of a red dot and two parallel white lines—along with a shaft that leans away from the target, the opposite of Dandy's shaft.

Odyssey's popular 2-Ball line features a pair of golf ball–size white circles behind the face to help alignment. The company Yes! Golf makes putters with grooves in the face. And Heavy Putter, as you may have guessed, makes clubs that weigh more.

And that's not counting the number of different styles and sizes from other manufacturers. For a more in-depth look at different types of putters and how they match your stroke, read on to the lessons.

If you already have a putter you love, get to the practice green and roll some putts. Although there are many different putters and varying ways to putt, there is one constant: You won't be a better putter without practice.

MARK'S LESSONS

Just as in the full swing, there is no single method that works best in putting. That's why there are so many different types of putters out there. It can get confusing, so in lieu of lessons based on ability, here's an overview of the different putter options and the effects they each have on strokes. After reading these descriptions, you should be able to make an informed decision the next time you're in the market for a flat stick.

LONG PUTTERS

(48–52 INCHES LONG)

These clubs have been the favorites of players like Bernhard Langer, who suffered from the yips on short putts. With the yips, the small muscles of the hands take over through impact, twisting the putter head and sending shots off-line. Anchoring this club against the chest takes the small muscles out of the motion, promoting a straight roll. While putts roll straight with this club, many golfers find that they have a problem with distance control.

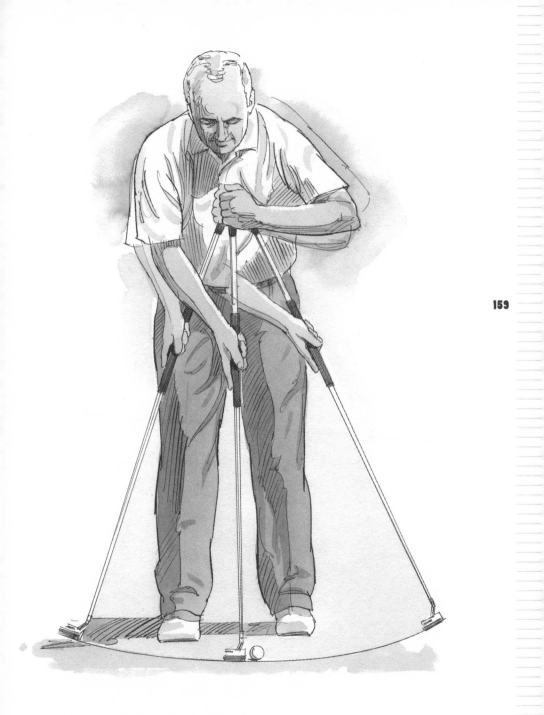

DANDY PUTTERS: MORE THAN ONE WAY TO GET THE BALL IN THE HOLE

MID-LENGTH PUTTERS

(39–45 INCHES LONG)

Also known as belly putters, mid-length putters allow you to anchor the club against your body while still using your normal stroke. On tour, this putter has been popular among top players looking for help on the greens, and its highest-profile practitioners have included Vijay Singh, Sergio Garcia, and Angel Cabrera, who at the 2009 Masters became the first player to win a major using a longer putter.

While this putter has helped players with their strokes and is worth a try if you're struggling, be aware that because the club is fixed against your body, proper length and lie are crucial. If it doesn't fit properly, you won't be able to use it effectively and it can actually do more harm than good.

The keys are to get the length right so you're using your normal setup and to then match the lie angle to your setup so the putter is soled flat against the ground. A toe-up position will promote putts that go to the left, while a heel-up position sends the ball to the right.

Because the end of the shaft is fixed against your body, the club will move in a natural pendulum motion. And unless the shaft is straight up and down, this fulcrum-based action will cause an inside-square-inside stroke. So if you're looking for a straight-back, straight-through path, the belly putter may not be for you.

||||||||||||||||||||||||||||||| **DANDY PUTTERS: MORE THAN ONE WAY TO GET THE BALL IN THE HOLE**

CONVENTIONAL-LENGTH PUTTERS

(33–36 INCHES LONG)

The length you choose has everything to do with your setup: how tall you stand and how you like to hang your arms. If your setup positions your eyes directly over the target line and aligns the putter face squarely, the length of the putter is secondary.

HAND POSITION

Most putters have shafts that are perfectly perpendicular to the ground when the head is soled flat on the ground. But recently, there have been putters with shafts that lean either slightly toward the target or away from it.

Dandy putters have shafts that lean toward the target, a feature that I like because I want my students to hit putts with their hands ahead of the ball. I feel that this position promotes a true roll. A putter with offset, where the shaft is in front of the clubface, also helps you keep your hands ahead of the ball.

IIIIIIIIIIIIIIIIIIIIIIIIIIIIIIIIIIIII **DANDY PUTTERS: MORE THAN ONE WAY TO GET THE BALL IN THE HOLE**

PUTTER HEAD

There are two main types of putter heads: blades and mallets. Blades, like the Ping Anser, are the most popular, while mallets, like the Odyssey Two-Ball, are gaining in market share. Whichever you choose is a matter of what fits your eye (the putter's shape, alignment) and feel (its weight).

From a stroke-shape perspective, the more important variable is where the shaft meets the head. If it is near the heel, the putter works better with an arc stroke in which it moves inside the target line in the backstroke and follow-through. Center-shafted putters are for players who make a straight-back, straight-through stroke.

FACE INSERTS

Beyond the factors mentioned above, there are other options among putters, namely face inserts and grip. Both affect feel and are largely personal preferences. If you want putts to feel softer (mostly due to the sound), go for an insert that muffles impact. Inserts also allow manufacturers to move more weight to the heel and toe, which increases the size of the sweet spot and makes the putter more forgiving.

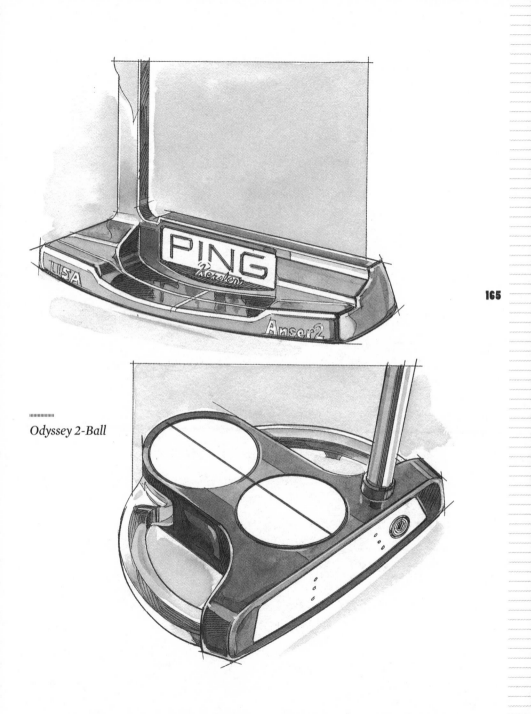

Odyssey 2-Ball

165

HARVEY PENICK

Bottom of the Arc

My lasting image of Harvey Penick is that of him sitting on his golf cart, his legs hanging off the side, on the driving range at Austin Country Club. He would always be in front of his pupil, and sometimes I would offer to move his cart around so he could have a different view of his student's swing. He might want to look at the player's swing plane, for instance.

But Harvey would always decline, because he wanted to see the bottom of the swing arc. In fact, nobody studied that part of the swing more than Harvey did. He also studied divots, which were a reflection of where the bottom of the arc took place. Those two aspects of the swing told him everything he needed to know about the shot.

The man couldn't see more than ten feet in front of him, but he could tell exactly where the ball went from the bottom of the arc and the divot. Long before video and launch monitors, there was Harvey, looking at divots and determining exactly the ball's trajectory. He was like a tracker who could read footprints in the forest.

His approach made sense. Because if you really think about it, impact is the only part of the swing that matters. Simply put, if you can improve your impact position, you will hit better shots.

While the prevailing wisdom is that most players' practice swings are better than their motions on the actual course, Harvey thought otherwise. Sure, most practice swings look prettier and have better rhythm. But when Harvey looked at the rehearsal swings, he saw that many of them bottomed well behind the ball, which meant that all these players were doing was practicing a swing that would produce fat shots. And many others missed the ground entirely, the club moving upward at impact, which meant they were practicing thin shots.

The clubhead of an iron needs to be moving down slightly at impact, so it bottoms out just on the target side of the ball and produces a shallow divot that starts in front of the ball. Different faults produce different divots. Players who swing too much from the inside bottom out behind the ball. Players with outside-in swings have overly steep paths and produce deep divots.

The next time you're at the driving range, try the following experiment: Draw a line in the grass and make some swings, trying to start the back of the divot at the line. It may seem easy to do, but it really isn't.

And there is more to divots than where they start. One day, Harvey explained to me how to read divots. A divot's location, shape, and depth tell us a lot about the swing and what the clubhead was doing at impact.

The ideal location for a divot is just on the target side of the ball. Divots that start too far behind indicate a fat shot and a loss of distance. In addition, the divot should line up directly along the target line, which indicates square contact. A divot that is inside the target line means contact was toward the toe, while a divot to the outside indicates heel impact.

The shape of a divot is also important. Byron Nelson, who hit the ball dead straight, produced divots that looked like dollar bills, which meant that he kept the club square and moving down the target line for a long time. Ben Hogan's divot holes looked like shrimp, curving off to the left, which made perfect sense because his preferred shot shape was a fade. Conversely, a player who hooks the ball would have a divot that flies to the right. So make sure the shape matches the shot you want to hit.

Harvey also told me to look at the divot's depth, which is largely overlooked. A deep hole means the player has a steep swing; golfers with shallow swings make shallow divot holes and sometimes don't even take any turf.

Divots also aren't always consistently deep. A divots that is deeper toward the toe indicates a club with a lie angle that is too flat. Conversely, divots that are consistently deeper toward the heel may mean that the lie angle is too upright. Changing the lie angle doesn't always fix the problem, but it will go a long way toward promoting straighter shots.

Harvey was able to diagnose faults from a small patch of dirt, and for most students, the fix was simple. Instead of filling his students' heads with complicated swing theories or images, he usually told them to try to clip the ball off a tee to move the bottom of their swings.

If their swings were too flat, the drill automatically would put the swing on the right plane. If the student swung over the top, it would fix that, too. Harvey knew that if you could clip the ball off a tee consistently, the bottom of your swing would be at the right place in the swing: just ahead of the ball.

Even when you're hitting a driver off a tee, the location of the swing's bottom is important. While you want a slightly descending path with an iron, the ideal driver swing path should be the opposite: The clubhead should be ascending slightly at impact. This will help you hit the ball higher and put less backspin on it, which allows you to get the maximum carry distance on your drives. In addition, you will get more roll.

If your driver is descending at impact, your shots will have too much backspin. You will hit the ball too low and not carry as far. Plus, you will get little roll, making your drives even shorter.

The obvious difference is that drivers don't make divots, so it's harder to read what's going on at impact. This is where technology has made a huge difference. Launch monitors provide precise numbers about driver impact.

Although primarily a club-fitting tool, the proper interpretation of launch numbers such as launch angle, backspin rate, and ball speed as a function of clubhead speed (known as "smash factor") can help teachers make changes in their students' swings. Even a small adjustment, such as teeing the ball a half inch higher on a tee, can have a significant effect on the ball's flight.

People think that to hit longer drives they need to swing faster. True, but a faster swing often makes it harder to hit the ball squarely on the sweet spot. Square contact with a slightly slower swing will usually hit the ball farther than off-center impact at a faster speed.

New technology may be helping teachers diagnose their students' swings, but whether you're using your eyes or a high-speed camera, the most important part of the golf swing remains impact.

MARK'S LESSONS

Although the basic shape of the swing is the same with every club, how the clubhead behaves at the bottom of the arc varies as you go through the bag.

Shaft length is crucial in determining the bottom of the arc. The driver has the longest shaft, which requires that you stand the farthest away from the ball and swing more around your body. The wedges and short irons have the shortest shafts, which means that you are standing closer to the ball and swinging more up than around. Here are some ways to make sure the bottom of the arc is exactly where you need it to be in order to hit good shots.

HIGH HANDICAPPER

At impact, the driver needs to be moving upward, which means the clubhead reaches the bottom of its arc when it is behind the ball. But too many high handicappers make contact before the clubhead reaches the bottom, so that it is moving down, not up.

This contact is the result of a steep, out-to-in swing and produces weak slices. To correct, start by adjusting your address position.

Pay particular attention to several aspects of your setup: weight distribution, ball position, and spine angle. A poor address position often dooms beginners before they even start their swings. They have too much weight on the left foot (for right-handed golfers), which moves the bottom of the swing forward. Their ball position is too far back in the stance, which compounds the previous error.

At address with a driver, the player should favor the right side, so approximately 60 percent of his or her weight is over the back foot. This will move the bottom of the arc back. The player should then tee the ball higher and position the ball somewhere opposite the left foot. Finally, the player should tilt his or her upper body away from the target slightly so the right shoulder is lower than the left.

These adjustments will help shallow out your swing path so the clubhead reaches the bottom of its arc behind the ball and impact is solid, producing longer drives.

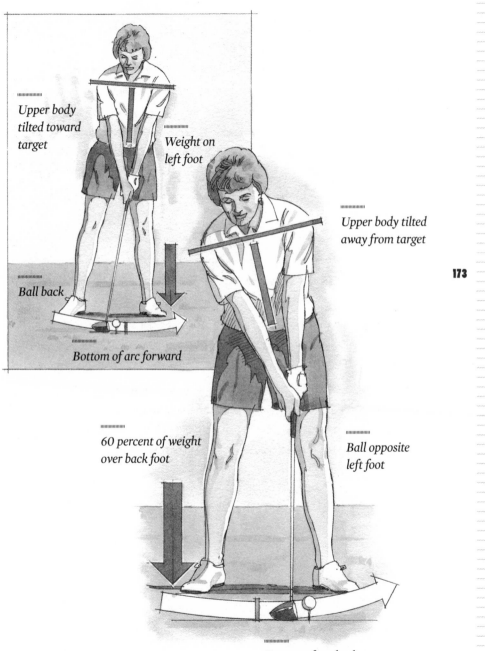

Upper body
tilted toward
target

Weight on
left foot

Upper body tilted
away from target

Ball back

Bottom of arc forward

60 percent of weight
over back foot

Ball opposite
left foot

Bottom of arc back

MID HANDICAPPER

The mid and short irons are the scoring clubs, and you need to hit them on the green consistently in order to make the pars and birdies that will take you to the next level. If your swing seems sound, and your contact is solid, but you still miss a lot of green, especially to the left or right, look at your divots.

With scoring clubs, divot holes should either be straight or curved slightly to the left. If they are markedly to the left or right, alignment may be your problem. Even if you have a good swing, you have to aim at the target for the ball to travel in the right direction.

Also look at the divot holes' depths, which should be uniform. Chances are that either the toe or the heel side is deeper, which indicates that the club's shaft length and/or lie angle does not fit with your swing. This isn't surprising, considering that the vast majority of golfers use standard clubs but don't have average specs.

Using a club with the wrong lie angle for your height and arm length can affect the direction of your shots. If your lie angle is too upright, the toe of the club will be up at impact. The clubhead will have a tendency to close, sending shots to the left. If the lie angle is too flat, the heel will be up and the ball will go right.

In either case, fixing the lie angle so the sole glides through the ball evenly will help you hit the ball straighter. You can work with a club fitter to make sure your lie angle is correct, but the path to improvement starts by examining your divots.

Straight

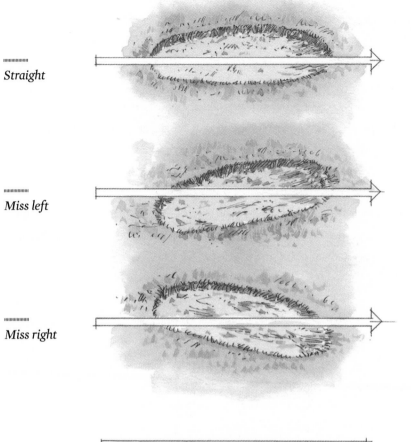

Miss left

Miss right

Uniform depth

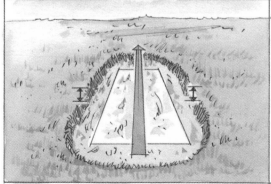

LOW HANDICAPPER

Having the hands ahead of the ball is best for good iron play. This leans the shaft forward and compresses the ball for longer, straighter shots. It also usually results in sizeable divots.

But with wedge play, overdoing this hands-forward impact position isn't necessarily what you want. When hitting a wedge, the goal isn't distance but control, and having your hands excessively forward makes these precise shots difficult to hit.

First, it delofts the wedge too much, so balls fly farther than you may want. Second, this position imparts a lot of spin on the ball, making it behave erratically upon landing. When hitting a pitch, you need to judge both how far you want to fly it and how the shot rolls out upon landing. Ideally, you want it to take a short hop or two then roll out gradually. So if you're facing a fifty-five-yard shot, you know that you can hit a pitch with a fifty-yard carry and count on five yards of bounce and roll.

But a shot hit with too much spin can cause the ball either to sit tightly upon landing or even to spin back. This unpredictability makes it hard to get up and down consistently.

In addition, sometimes you will want to hit a high, soft-landing pitch, whether to an elevated green, a firm green, or a hole cut close to the edge of the green. You can't do that if your hands are too far ahead of the ball and your swing path is too steep.

How do you know if the path of your wedge is too steep? By looking at the divots, of course. You want to avoid a divot hole that is too deep. Try to hit wedges that have shallow divots, similar to the ones you produce with mid irons. This will give you more control over your pitch shots, so that you will make more pars and birdies.

*Positioning hands
too far ahead of
the ball delofts club*

*Positioning hands
slightly ahead of the
ball fosters greater
precision*

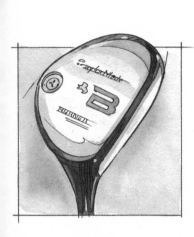

THE ENGINEERS

Golf as Science

For most of its history, golf has been more art than science. The best players were shot makers such as Bobby Jones and Ben Hogan, who could create beautiful shots with every club in the bag. The early club makers were craftsmen such as Allan Robertson and Old Tom Morris, who would painstakingly manufacture brassies and niblicks in their shops. Nowadays, these clubs from the nineteenth century are as valuable as fine art.

For more than a hundred years, golf clubs didn't change much. Even through the 1980s, woods were made of wood, and irons were forged by hand, the way they had been for decades. Then in the past twenty years or so, the science of golf equipment took off like a space shuttle launch. The metaphor is especially apt because much of the same technology used in rocket science has been applied to golf equipment.

Now the effort that goes into designing and producing golf clubs and balls involves multiple disciplines of science, including physics, metallurgy, and chemistry. And in place of a workbench, equipment companies have built large research centers where scientists perfect the design of clubs down to the last millimeter.

Clubs are now made of titanium and terms such as "center of gravity," "moment of inertia," and "perimeter weighting" have become commonplace in the golf lexicon. The size of the driver clubhead has more than doubled. In addition, these clubs have odd shapes—I can only imagine what Sam Snead would have thought of a square driver like the one Lucas Glover used to win the 2009 U.S. Open. Finally, new types of clubs like hybrids, which have replaced long irons, have changed the way people play golf.

Another advance is the customization of a club to fit a player's swing. Just a few years ago, the only options available for a driver were loft, shaft length, and shaft flex. A golfer who wanted to change any of those variables had to try a new club.

Nowadays, adjustable clubs allow players to change a club's loft, face angle, and weighting—and even switch shafts with a wrench. All of this technology was recently developed inside the top-secret research centers of the major equipment companies.

I have had the great fortune not only to get a look inside these high-tech chambers, but also to talk shop with golf's most brilliant scientists. My first such visit was in 1999, thanks to Richard C. Helmstetter, the brains behind the products produced by Callaway. In 1991, Helmstetter and Callaway revolutionized the golf equipment industry by introducing the Big Bertha, an oversize driver that had a larger sweet spot and was easier to hit than a wooden club. It was the first step on a voyage that has taken the golf world to the gigantic drivers that are commonplace today.

Although I was convinced that Helmstetter had dialed the wrong number, I accepted his invitation to fly out to California and visit Callaway's research center in Carlsbad, located just north of San Diego.

The technology was impressive. It was fascinating to see how the development teams designed the equipment by computer, and tested it in wind tunnels and other controlled environments. The biggest eye-opener was Callaway's launch monitors, which are commonplace now but were just beginning to impact the equipment business ten years ago. These monitors used high-speed cameras to capture precise images of the club and ball at impact.

For the first time, we were able to receive data on exactly what the club and ball were doing: information like the clubhead's speed, the angle of attack, and whether it was traveling from inside the target line or outside of it at impact. We also could calculate the ball's speed, launch angle, and spin.

And we could see how these different variables affected the ball's performance. Obviously, a driver with more loft would produce a higher launch angle. And a lighter shaft would increase clubhead speed. It would have seemed obvious that the higher the clubhead speed, the higher the ball speed and the longer the drive. But the launch monitors showed that sometimes a shot hit with lower clubhead speed would also produce longer drives.

When I was learning to play golf and for most of my golf career, the prevailing thought was that a low, penetrating drive produced the most distance off the tee. We wanted to avoid hitting high drives that would balloon and get caught in the wind. But the launch monitor showed that to hit the ball farther, golfers should hit their tee shots much higher. At the time, most golfers, even pros, hit drives with a launch angle of five to seven degrees. The monitor showed that most players achieved maximum distance when they launched at ten to twelve degrees. Compared to what we had been hitting, a twelve-degree drive looked like a pop-up.

But that wasn't all. In addition to launching the ball higher, players needed to minimize the ball's spin. A ball with too much spin would upshoot and fall to the ground like a stone, while less spin would help the ball to carry longer and roll more upon landing. Over the past ten years, the key to longer drives has been summed up in four words: high launch, low spin.

Where impact occurs on the driver's face has affects both. Driver faces are not flat; they are curved, especially near the edges. The curve from side to side is known as bulge, and the curve from top to bottom is roll.

Bulge and roll add spin to the shot through a phenomenon known as gear effect. Shots hit toward the toe have more hook spin; heel shots have slice spin. Balls hit near the bottom of the driver have more backspin, while shots hit above the center have less backspin. So we quickly learned to tee the ball high to maximize distance.

Based on the data collected by these scientists, companies began building clubs that were weighted, so shots would produce less spin. If a student comes to me looking for more distance, I recommend a club with more loft—at least ten degrees—and encourage the student to tee the ball higher. This combination will help maximize distance.

Nowadays, launch monitors are common, and many fitters have replaced their camera-based units with a system that uses Doppler radar to track the shot from beginning to end. This technology helps golfers make the best club selection from the numerous choices. These monitors can also help players pick the best type of ball for their games, by studying how the balls perform off the tee, off irons, and with short-game shots.

But no matter how sophisticated the technology, it is useless unless the user can apply it properly. Although the best club makers no longer produce clubs by hand, there is no substitute for the human factor. At Callaway's testing center, I was able to learn from some of the best minds in golf: Helmstetter, Roger Cleveland, Paul Runyan, Dave Pelz, and Alastair Cochran.

In 1979 Cleveland started in the golf business by making replicas of classic golf clubs from the 1940s and 1950s, and his namesake company soon became known for its wedges. When he went to Callaway, Cleveland brought with him his expertise as one of the best club designers in the industry.

Paul Runyan, known as Little Poison, won the 1934 and 1938 PGA Championships with one of the best short games in golf history. Later, he became a short-game instructor, who counted among his students Mickey Wright, Gene Littler, and Phil Rodgers (who in turn helped Jack Nicklaus with his chipping and putting).

Pelz, of course, is a short-game guru who approaches what many consider the most artful part of golf in a studied, methodical manner. He backs up his sound teaching methods with research collected over decades of watching both the pros and amateurs.

When it came to a scientific approach to golf, Cochran was well ahead of the curve. His book *Search for the Perfect Swing*, published in 1968, used physics to break down and analyze the complex movements of a golf swing. Before becoming a consultant for Callaway, he was the technical director for the Royal and Ancient Golf Club of St. Andrews, golf's ruling body outside the United States and Mexico.

That was a lot of intelligence under one roof, and I used the opportunity to pick their brains about the subtleties of their respective specialties. I'll never forget one conversation I had with Cleveland, Cochran, and Pelz.

An Englishman, Cochran was talking about how, back in Europe, players had a little trick for putting more spin on the ball on pitch shots. They would take a practice swing in an old divot so the grooves would fill with dirt. The theory was that the dirt made for a rough surface that would grab the ball and impart more spin. Controlling spin is the key to hitting precise shots.

Cochran pointed out that it was illegal to do this purposefully, since it meant the player was changing the playing characteristics of the club during the round. But proving this intent was next to impossible because the player simply was making a practice swing.

During my time at Callaway, I also learned that science doesn't always have all the answers. Later that same day, I asked the group, "What direction does the ball go out of greenside bunkers: the direction of the sand splashing or where the clubface is pointing?"

I had my own opinion about the topic: For the most part, the ball follows the sand. It may go slightly to the right depending on the coarseness of the sand and how far behind the ball your sand wedge enters the sand, but I always thought clubface alignment meant little.

I'd given a number of clinics on bunker play where I had illustrated this point by hitting shots from a variety of clubface positions. The ball would end up in the same place no matter how open I held the face.

The scientists were evenly split on this topic. Some thought the clubface influenced shot direction, while others agreed with my view. From this dissension, I came to the conclusion that while science is important in golf, it doesn't always explain the entire game. After all, the game is about results.

There are many cases when the shots you hit won't agree with the theory. For example, when hitting a shot with the ball below your feet, the physics say that the ball will fly to the right (for a right-handed player). So we instruct our students to aim to the left and allow for the tendency. But I can't tell you how many times I have seen players pull the ball well left of the green from that type of lie. Instead of blindly following theory, I have found that it is best to experiment to see which method works for each individual.

Several years later, I became a member of TaylorMade's professional staff and had the opportunity to work with another brilliant golf scientist: Benoit Vincent, TaylorMade's chief designer. Benoit's strength is his ability to take a difficult concept and make it simple for those of us without advanced engineering degrees.

I first talked to him right after TaylorMade purchased the Maxfli ball company and he was charged with making the best golf ball on the market. He explained how golf balls were made, and how a ball's construction and performance determined which ball I should use.

He explained that most balls have three main components: core, mantle, and cover. Usually made of rubber, the core is the ball's engine and plays the largest role in distance. The cover has the biggest effect on the shot's spin and feel around the greens. And the balls used by tour pros have an extra layer, called the mantle, between the core and cover, that can help any performance characteristic.

Through the work of scientists like Helmstetter and Vincent, the sport has evolved. And my interaction with these men showed me how to employ modern advances to help my students improve their games.

MARK'S LESSONS

More than ever, equipment can help golfers lower their scores. Engineers have made individual clubs easier to hit, developed new types of clubs, and customized features of clubs to fit each player like a bespoke suit. Here is how the advances by golf's best minds can help each playing level.

HIGH HANDICAPPER

The most important decision you can make in terms of equipment is set makeup. Here are the clubs I recommend:

Drivers: It should have a minimum of ten degrees of loft—I might even go higher, to twelve or thirteen degrees. This will help you to get the ball into the air and to hit the ball as far as you can. And don't choose a shaft that's longer than forty-four inches. The shorter the shaft, the easier the club is to hit.

Fairway woods and hybrids: These clubs, especially the hybrids, should make up the majority of your set because of how often you use them. Stock up on hybrids, which are easier to hit than irons and are more versatile from all sorts of lies. In fact, the longest iron you should have in the bag is a five-iron. Anything longer is too hard to hit.

Irons: As I stated above, a five-iron is all you need. Look for perimeter-weighted clubs with thick soles because their center of gravity is lower in the clubhead, allowing you to get the ball in the air much more easily.

Wedges: While lob wedges are popular on tour, they do more harm than good in the hands of high handicappers. Instead, trade in that sixty-degree lob wedge for a gap wedge, which has about fifty-two degrees of loft. You'll get a lot more use out of it.

Putters: As you should for an iron, look for a putter with perimeter weighting, which gives the putter a bigger sweet spot and makes it more forgiving when you miss that spot. Those mishits are the biggest reason for three-putts, so you should try to eliminate that mistake as much as possible.

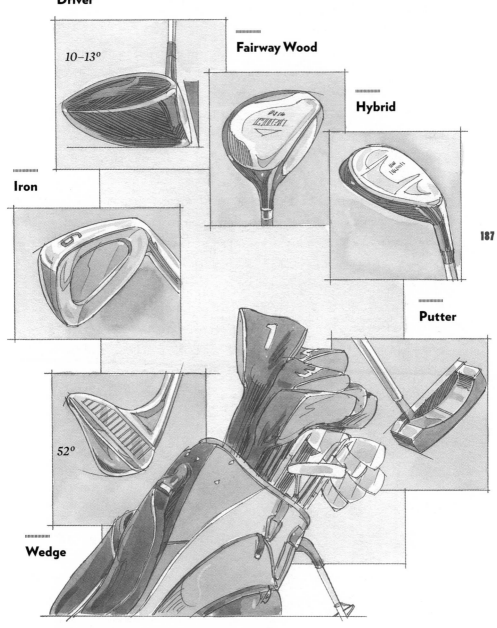

$10–13º$

Fairway Wood

Hybrid

Iron

187

Putter

$52º$

Wedge

MID HANDICAPPER

There is only one piece of equipment that you use on every shot. Which makes your choice of a ball one of the most important decisions you can make.

TaylorMade's Benoit Vincent believes that since so many strokes take place around the green, the important part of choosing a ball is how it feels and performs on pitches and chips. I agree. In general, I recommend that my students buy balls that have soft covers, which will enable them to get the most out of their short game. They might give up a few yards off the tee, but not enough to have a negative impact on their scores.

The balls used by tour players usually have firm cores. Activating the core by compressing it with the club is the key to hitting longer drives. Unfortunately, most golfers don't swing fast enough to do this to the fullest.

At the same time, these tour balls feel soft and have enough spin on wedge shots to satisfy even short-game wizards like Phil Mickelson. Balls that are long off the tee yet feel soft have been the biggest difference in golf balls over the past ten years. Not long ago, there were only two types of balls. Soft models with balata covers had the best feel, but they spun a lot and didn't go as far. The other choice was at the opposite end of the spectrum: so-called rocks traveled longer but offered little feel or spin around the greens.

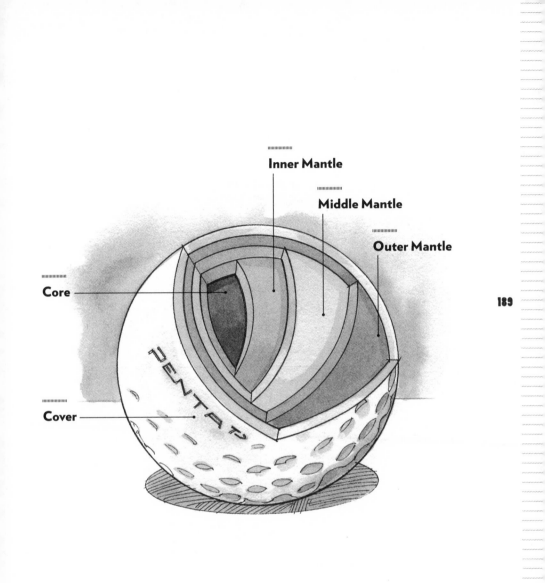

Inner Mantle

Middle Mantle

Outer Mantle

Core

Cover

LOW HANDICAPPER

Until recently, buying a driver was relatively simple. You would pick a demo driver with a head that you liked in the shaft flex and that fit your swing speed, and you would hit some balls with it. If the ball flight was to your liking, you'd buy the driver.

The process today is more complicated. There are clubhead options available in loft, face angle, and head weighting. Specific combinations promote different shot shapes. And if you can't decide which you prefer, there are now clubs that you can adjust to your liking from day to day.

And that's not even counting the scores of different shafts. The bad news is that there are hundreds of different combinations available, and that can be confusing.

The good news is that a formula can be found that is perfect for you and will enable you to gain as many as twenty yards from your current driver. This optimization is one of the reasons tour pros have been hitting the ball so far.

If you want to get the most out of your game, get fitted for a driver using a launch monitor. The trained fitters know all the options and can quickly narrow down the choices for you. They'll then allow you to test each club and find out which performs best for you.

There is no better confidence builder than knowing that your driver is the one best suited for your swing. And confident swings result in long, straight shots. That's the kind of science that has really transformed golf.

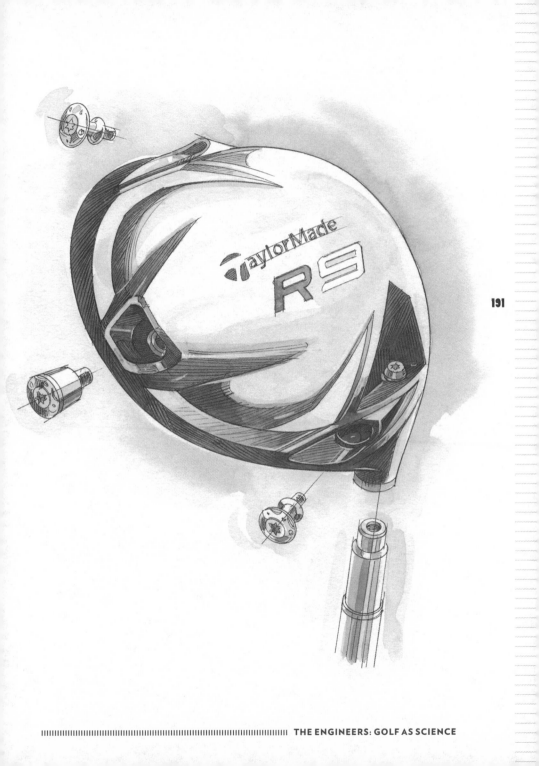

191

MICHAEL JORDAN

Playing in the Clutch

The question is asked every day in sports bars around the country: "Who is the greatest athlete ever?" There is no shortage of candidates, from Jim Thorpe to Jesse Owens to Babe Ruth to Jim Brown to Michael Jordan to Tiger Woods. There are strong arguments for all them, but my vote goes to Jordan.

Of course, my choice isn't completely objective: The day I spent playing golf against him has influenced it. You would have thought that as a golf instructor, I would have a lot to teach an amateur golfer. But it turned out that Jordan had more to show me.

Jordan's greatness was due to more than his athletic ability. True, he had tremendous skills. But so did a lot of other players, who could jump as high, dunk as acrobatically, shoot as accurately, and defend as tenaciously. The difference was that no other player wanted to win as much as Jordan did. And the larger the stage, the better he played.

I had a glimpse into Jordan's competitive nature when I spent a few days in Chicago in 1996 with Ed Ibarguen, the head professional at the Duke University Golf Club in Durham, North Carolina. Before going to Duke, Ed worked at the University of North Carolina's Finley Golf Course, where he gave lessons to Jordan and later befriended him.

While in Chicago, Ed arranged for us to watch a couple of Bulls games. We did more than spectate. We were able to go into the locker room, received the best table at Jordan's restaurant, and even watched a special screening of *Space Jam*, the cartoon movie starring several NBA stars, including Jordan.

After the first game, Ed and I met up with Jordan. He offered us tickets for the following night's game but warned, "You probably don't want to come. It won't be much fun for you, since it won't be much of a game."

Right then, I realized how much Jordan loves a challenge. He plays for the chance to elevate his game to match a worthy opponent and often performs at his best in the play-offs or in late-game pressure situations, when the outcome is in doubt.

It is easy to think that basketball came easily for Jordan, but the truth is that he had to overcome obstacles. Far from being a phenom, Jordan was cut from his high school team as a sophomore. Instead of giving up, he worked harder to make the team the next year.

At the University of North Carolina, he would play Ping-Pong and billiards with teammates. Although he was a beginner, he kept asking for rematches until he finally won a game.

Golf is perfect for Jordan because it is impossible to conquer. It feeds his love of competition. I was on the receiving end of Jordan's zeal about ten years after I had watched him play in Chicago. He came to my club, Carlton Woods, to play thirty-six holes in a single day.

The mind games started early, even before we got to the first tee. We were negotiating the bet and I asked him about the amount of the wager. "Whatever makes you nervous" was his reply.

For the rest of the day, his trash talking was relentless. He tried to get under my skin on nearly every shot. When I hit a poor shot, he would say something like, "You call yourself a pro with that shot? Wait till I tell my friends I beat the pro at his own club."

After a while, I started to think about what he would say and how I would respond instead of focusing on my shot. Jordan had accomplished his mission of getting in my head and throwing me off my game.

Conversely, he never seemed to get ruffled, no matter what I said or did.

Although he hit his share of bad shots, he was confident in everything he did. I may have been the better player, but you would never have known it from his body language.

And when I gave him grief in return, Jordan gave me a look that said, "Do you know who you're messing with? You don't want any part of this." The only other person who had given me that look on the course was another pretty good competitor, Jack Nicklaus.

And like Nicklaus, Jordan played better as the pressure increased. During our first round, he played so-so for the first fourteen holes. But as we came to the last several holes, he found another gear.

We were playing a game called "Wolf." In this four-player game, a different player is designated the wolf on each hole. The wolf tees off first, then chooses a partner after the others have hit. The wolf and his partner then play against the remaining two players—two on two—for the hole. The better score of either player on each team counts.

In general, the wolf picks the best player or the one who has hit the best drive on the hole. But the wolf also has the option of playing the hole alone against the others—one on three. That means that in order to win the hole, the wolf's score has to be better than those of the other three players—tough odds.

The fifteenth hole of our Nicklaus course is a long par-four of 455 yards from the back tee. It is one of the most difficult holes, and Jordan was the wolf.

He hit the fairway. Two others in the group, including me, hit longer tee shots. But Jordan decided that it was time to make the other players nervous. Despite his disadvantageous position, he chose to play the hole without a partner.

As he surveyed the shot of more than two hundred yards, his body language seemed different. He stood taller, his focus seemed sharper, and his movements were more deliberate. While most of us speed up our minds and bodies under pressure, Jordan did the opposite.

I'm sure much of his aplomb had to do with his ability to draw from his experiences on the basketball court. After all, he had made numerous baskets in the last seconds, starting with his game-winning jump shot as a freshman for North Carolina in the 1982 NCAA Championship game against George-town. First-year players normally don't get the ball in those situations, but his coach, the legendary Dean Smith, obviously realized that even at the age of nineteen, Jordan was mentally strong.

So it didn't surprise me when Jordan hit his best shot of the day on that fifteenth hole. The ball finished just two feet from the hole—an easy birdie. He looked at me, winked, and asked if I'd heard him coming. Then, as I was walking to my ball to hit my second shot, he continued the trash talking: "There's no stopping me now." "Are you nervous?" "Would you like to buy out of the bet now?"

Not surprisingly, I hit a poor shot and Jordan won the hole. I can only imagine what he would say on the court as he played the game in which he was the world's best. Even though I was the better golfer, his supreme confidence and extreme competitive spirit were able to lift his game above mine.

Playing against Jordan is difficult. Being on the same side of this intensity is fun, yet carries a burden. He wants to win so much that as his partner, you don't want to let him down. The experience gave me some perspective into what Jordan's teammates, like Scottie Pippen, no doubt felt every night.

The pressure motivated me to play better. In that way, Jordan improved the quality of the play all around, and I could easily see how his Chicago Bulls had become one of the best teams in sports history.

It is one thing to watch him drive to the basket, dunk, and make a fade-away shot. But until you have faced him as a competitor, you truly do not get the entire sense of what makes Jordan the best athlete in the world.

MARK'S LESSONS

Every golf club has one: a player with a good-looking swing who stripes the ball on the driving range but can't do much once he gets on the course. Chances are, he spends a lot of time grooving his swing but neglects the mental part of playing golf, namely the ability to perform under pressure.

Ocassionally when there are a few members practicing, I go out to the range and make them an offer. I point to a target green about 125 yards away and ask them to hit five balls on the green. If they make all five, they'll receive a dozen balls from the shop. If they miss, they have to run laps around the range.

Ordinarily, for most, hitting this green is no problem. It's just a smooth wedge. I have seen many of them hit ten or more balls on the green while practicing. But when bad shots have a consequence, it's a different story. They look uncomfortable and rush their swings. More often than not, they end up running.

Good competitors aren't fazed by these situations. And the best competitors, like Michael Jordan, play even better. The key is to practice situations in which nerves play a part in affecting the outcome of the shot.

HIGH HANDICAPPER

Good competitors are comfortable in stressful situations. Often, I can sense when players are feeling the heat by the way they address the ball.

You can ease the stress by developing a reliable, repeatable pre-shot routine that you perform the same way before every swing on the course: Line up the shot from behind the ball, take a practice swing, step into your address position, and make sure you are aligned correctly before you take the swing.

A pre-shot routine ensures that you are relaxed and in the right mind frame for the shot. Develop a routine, then be disciplined about sticking to it.

THE PRE-SHOT
ROUTINE

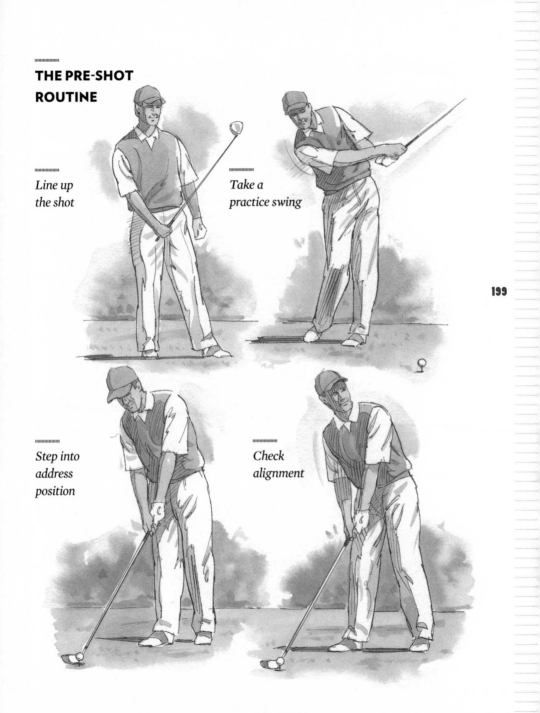

*Line up
the shot*

*Take a
practice swing*

*Step into
address
position*

*Check
alignment*

MID HANDICAPPER

When you practice, don't just beat balls mindlessly. In addition to honing the physical side of your game, work on your competitive skills. Just as I do with my members, set a challenge for yourself on the range.

Try to hit five greens in a row. Try to hit five "fairways" in a row by hitting drives between flags on the range. On the practice green, try to sink ten three-footers in a row. The key is to ratchet up the pressure with each successful shot.

Most important, there should be a consequence if you miss. If you can't make ten straight putts, leave a dollar bill in the cup. A penalty for failure should be enough motivation to handle the anxiety of the situation successfully.

LOW HANDICAPPER

Tour pros can play a lot of different shots, but when the pressure is on, all of them have a reliable go-to shot. Tiger Woods has his "stinger," a low, piercing long iron off the tee that doesn't travel far, but almost always winds up in the short grass.

This shot is akin to a second serve in tennis, a shot designed to get the ball in play, no more. It should be immune to the nerves that build up in pressure situations. The most likely shape for such a shot is a fade, because it is easier to hit.

Set up on the right side of the tee box and aim down the left edge of the fairway. In the downswing, keep your hands quiet to keep the club from closing through impact. The open face will cause a shot that starts left where you are aiming before curving right and landing in the fairway. But as with any other shot, practice before you try it on the course.

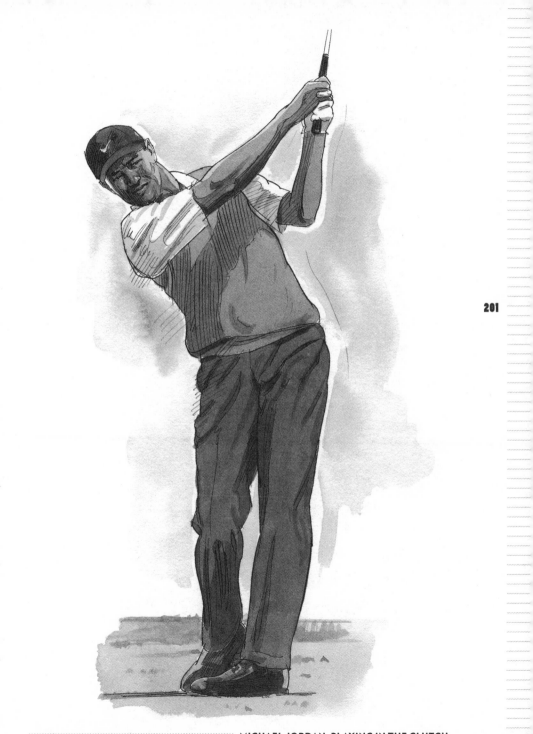

MICHAEL JORDAN: PLAYING IN THE CLUTCH

LESSON 21

ROLAND THATCHER
Tour Guide

One of my favorite parts of teaching is sharing in the successes and achievements of my students, whether it's watching them hit the ball in the air for the first time, listening as they recount their first birdie, or watching as they make a putt to break 80 for the first time.

But I have to admit that there is no thrill quite like watching one of your students play at the highest level of the game: the PGA Tour. I have been fortunate enough to work with several tour players, but only one of them has been my student since his junior golf days.

I met Roland Thatcher in the mid 1990s while I was running my golf school at the TPC Woodlands outside Houston. He was a junior in high school and was being recruited by several Division I schools. (He wound up choosing Auburn University in Alabama, where he won the individual Southeastern Conference Championship as a senior in 2000.)

Although Roland wasn't tall, he was built solidly, like a linebacker. On the golf course, he was also as aggressive as one. Because of his style of play, Roland made a lot of birdies, and when he was in the groove, he broke some course records. But that aggressive play had a downside; when his risks didn't work out, he made many double bogeys.

Roland's swing path back then was steep. Nobody took bigger divots than Roland, which meant he hit his irons solidly. Like my friend Joel Edwards, Roland kept his hands ahead of the ball and trapped it. But that same action caused trouble around the green, especially from bunkers. His game was very rough around the edges, and I was excited about helping him harness his talent.

I was so confident about his potential that I offered to work with him free of charge through college and the mini-tours until he made it to the PGA Tour. It was a sacrifice, but I had no doubts that he would play at the game's highest level.

Besides all that talent, Roland has what I like to call a "golf brain," a player who rarely make mental errors on the course. And at each level he has played, from junior golf to college to mini-tours to the Nationwide Tour and now the PGA Tour, he has gotten smarter, making better decisions on the course.

Tour players have to make decisions that average players don't. In a crosswind, I would advise most players to simply aim left or right. But pros have to decide whether to shape their shot to ride the wind or hold it against the breeze, depending on which shot will land the ball closer to the hole.

Or they have to decide whether to hit a high shot that sits softly or a low approach that rolls out after hitting the ground. Players with golf brains always make the correct decisions in these situations.

Like any other part of the game, the golf brain improves with practice and experience. When he turned professional, Roland wasn't mentally prepared to play on the PGA Tour, but he nearly made it.

In 2001 he was playing the final stage of the Tour Qualifying School for the first time, at Bear Lakes Country Club in West Palm Beach. Q-School, as the event is known, is the country's most grueling test of golf. After surviving two four-round stages, contestants play for their careers during the six-round final. Only those who finish in the top twenty-five get to play for millions on the PGA Tour. The rest play for far less money on the Nationwide Tour.

That year, Roland came to the final hole needing to make par to earn a spot on the PGA Tour. He hit a drive into the rough, then misjudged his approach, hitting a flier that flew over the green. The ball bounced off a cart path and ended up on the clubhouse roof.

The tournament staff hadn't anticipated that happening, which meant they hadn't allowed for a drop area. Following the rules by the book, the nearest point of relief was a bush. From there, Roland had to take an unplayable lie and wound up making triple bogey.

Although he was devastated at the time, we now believe it was probably for the best that he didn't earn his card on his first try. He needed to play on the Nationwide Tour to develop his game, both physically and mentally.

The biggest change we needed to make was in his short game. I really didn't want him to change his full swing because he had such a good impact position and hit the ball so powerfully. As I've mentioned, some of golf's best ball-strikers—Ben Hogan, Johnny Miller, Phil Mickelson—had a dominant lead hand. After getting to know Roland, I wasn't surprised to learn that he hit a lot of shots with just his left hand when he was younger.

The goal was to make his steep, V-shaped swing more rounded, like a U with the short game. That way, he would come into more impact more consistently and with the same loft every time, so he could better control the trajectory and spin of the shots.

When a player makes his living covering the ball by trapping it against the turf, it is a tricky proposition to shallow out the swing on short shots without messing up the long game. So we spent a lot of time with Roland hitting short wedge shots with just his right hand. Taking a cue from Harvey Penick, I measured Roland's progress by his divots. As a teen, he used to take huge, deep divots that flew off to the right. But as his pitch-shot swing became more shallow, the divots became smaller, thinner, and pointed to the left.

Strangely, while injuries often hinder a player's progress, a back injury that caused Roland to take a few months off actually helped shallow out his swing. When he came back, he was more flexible, which enabled him to rotate better back and through the ball.

This rotation not only improved his short game, but also made his ball-striking more consistent. His shots weren't as explosive as before, but it helped

Roland's game in the long run. Eventually his physical prowess matched his golf brain, which had been developing as he played in more and more events against better and better competition.

In 2007 Roland won twice on the Nationwide Tour and finished second on the money list to earn a spot on the PGA Tour. He was playing much better on the 2008 PGA Tour, with two top-ten finishes, when he injured his wrist in the middle of the year. But he came back and had a second-place finish in 2009 and earned enough money to remain on the tour.

Roland has learned to play on the PGA Tour, and the main lesson I have learned while observing him both at home, while we're working on his game, and on tour, where I have caddied for him, is that mechanics don't have a place on the course once the tournament begins. In four rounds, he never said a word about his swing. Instead, the conversation was all about strategy and course management: all parts of his golf brain.

The best way to keep from thinking about mechanics is to work hard in practice to make swing changes feel completely intuitive. That sounds easy, but it is difficult to do. When Roland is home, we practice *not* thinking about mechanics by playing rounds in which I try to distract him. For instance, I'll talk nonstop during his swing to throw off his focus.

Early in the week, these distractions work, and I am sometimes able to beat him. But as the week progresses and the time for Roland to return to the tour draws closer, his focus intensifies and his competitive edge is finely honed. When it comes time for him to leave, he's winning every round.

Now that we have slowly adjusted his swing to where we want it, this sharpening of his golf brain is the best way I can help him prepare to play against the best players in the world.

MARK'S LESSONS

Golf is not necessarily about who has the best swing or hits the ball most solidly—although that helps a lot. It's about who has the mental ability to complement those physical skills.

What has enabled Roland Thatcher to advance to the PGA Tour, golf's highest level, has been the development of both sides of his golf game. Even if you can't hit the ball like Roland, you can get the most out of your game by developing your golf brain. Here's how.

HIGH HANDICAPPER

Although golf is often a competition against yourself or the course, much of the fun of the game comes from playing against other golfers. And most competitions are match-play events with handicaps factored in. Which means that holes are won by the player or team with the lower net score. And the side that wins the most holes wins the match.

For example, a twenty-five-handicap golfer playing against a seven-handicap receives eighteen shots during the round, or one per hole. That means that on each hole, one stroke is subtracted from the high-handicapper's score. In order to win the hole, the high-handicap player simply has to tie the low-handicap golfer.

The low-handicapper will have some bad holes, so the high handicapper needs to play intelligently and avoid big numbers to win. At the end of the day, using his or her golf brain will allow the high handicapper to be the one collecting the cash from the low-handicapper opponent.

MID HANDICAPPER

At this level, you have some control over your shots, and you can use that to your advantage to emphasize your strengths and downplay your weaknesses.

If you miss a lot of short putts of six feet and less, check your alignment, ball position, and whether your eyes are over the ball at address. Straighten out your path and keep your head still. But save those lessons for the practice green. When you're playing, focus on your pre-shot routine and rhythm.

And until you gain more confidence on short putts, avoid putting yourself in stressful situations. For example, if you have missed a green, it might be safer to hit a chip that leaves an uphill ten-footer instead of a tricky, downhill left-to-right four-footer. An uphill putt, even if it's longer, is easier to make.

209

Use this strategy for whichever weaknesses your game possesses. If you hit a slice and there's a water hazard down the right side, hit a fairway wood off the tee. Playing from the fairway, even from farther back, is better for your golf brain than the memory of another shot splashing into the water. Keep up the positive feedback and you'll become a better player in the long run.

LOW HANDICAPPER

What every good player can learn from Roland is his ability to separate the golf swing from playing golf. During off weeks, he doesn't hit a lot of balls. Instead he plays rounds to prepare for the PGA Tour.

He and I work on mechanics only during the winter, when he has more time to ingrain changes. I've seen many golfers do more harm than good by taking a swing-in-progress to the course. Instead of committing to the changes, they will respond to the shots they are hitting, abandoning what they are working on in order to hit better shots.

Tinkering with your swing while playing golf will distract you from the goal of managing your game and shooting a low score. So if you want to focus on your golf swing, do so on the practice tee. When you're on the course, simply play golf.

JACK NICKLAUS

Born Competitor

As fine a player as Jack Nicklaus was, he has become almost an equally accomplished golf course architect. His firm, Nicklaus Design, has built more than three hundred courses around the world, and his creations have been ranked among the world's best. The PGA Tour plays on several of his layouts, including Harbour Town Golf Links on Hilton Head Island in South Carolina; Muirfield Village Golf Club outside of his hometown of Columbus, Ohio; and Sherwood Country Club in Thousand Oaks, California. In addition, two of his courses, Shoal Creek Golf Club in Birmingham, Alabama, and Valhalla Golf Club in Louisville, Kentucky, have hosted two PGA Championships each. Certainly, it shouldn't be long before one of his creations hosts the U.S. Open.

Jack commands seven-figure fees for one of his signature designs, but the price tag usually includes an exhibition round at the course's grand opening. It's a terrific marketing tool for the club, and hundreds of club members and prospective members, property owners and prospective buyers, as well as local media, attend the opening, getting a rare, up-close opportunity to interact with Jack.

As he plays, he talks about the course and what he was thinking as he designed the holes. It's usually a ceremonial round, but given how competitive Jack is, the golf can become intense, as I personally found out.

Sometimes, he invites the host professional to play with him, and as the director of golf at The Club at Carlton Woods in The Woodlands, Texas, I had the honor of joining him at the grand opening of his course on June 5, 2001.

I had worked for the Nicklaus/Flick Golf Schools, but had never spent much time with Jack, certainly not nearly as much as I would spend with him that day. I had always been a big fan of his, and I couldn't wait to play with him—I was about to experience nearly every golfer's dream.

Jack has always been known for his precision and meticulous nature on the course: He was one of the first players to determine exact yardages for shots; before, players just eyeballed the approximate distance. He is the same way off the course, and so is his staff, who seemed to have planned out the day to the minute.

I worked with Scott Tolley, Jack's director of public relations, for months before the grand opening, and it didn't take me long to realize Jack and his company did things a little differently from everybody else. Jack doesn't like surprises; and he signed off on everything Scott and I arranged, from the exact time of his pickup at the airport, to the color of shirt he would wear, to the timing of his schedule, to whom he would meet when.

Luckily, our golf course superintendent, Eric Bauer, clued me in on how Jack operates before the job began. Eric had started his career in turfgrass by maintaining Jack's backyard tennis courts in Florida. From there, he had gone on to work at Shoal Creek, Manele Bay in Hawaii, and Spring Creek Ranch in Tennessee, before coming to Carlton Woods. Nobody I had ever met was more of a planner and a lover of challenges than Eric. Based on my dealings with Jack's company for the grand opening, I could see where Eric had picked up the qualities that make him among America's best superintendents.

Since Eric knew Jack well, I enlisted him to go with me to pick him up at a private airport about thirty minutes away. Air Bear, as Jack's Gulfstream V is affectionately known in the golf industry, landed right on time. It taxied to a stop, the door opened up, and the Golden Bear walked out.

As we said hello, I looked into those steel-blue eyes and could see why Scott Tolley had warned me that playing with Jack could turn a ten-handicapper into a twenty, and a twenty into a thirty. No doubt, it's the same way golfers feel when they play with Tiger Woods.

Many players say of playing in a major championship against Jack that he knows he's going to win, you know he's going to win, and he knows that you know he's going to win. That's the "Nicklaus factor," and from my brief experience with him, I'd say Jack seemed to enjoy this advantage.

We arrived at Carlton Woods just as the script had dictated, and Jack spent half an hour in my office stretching until he was ready. Like many golfers, Jack has back problems and undergoes a strict daily regimen. He simply was not going to the range until he had stretched, for which he had allotted thirty minutes, not a minute less—there was no ad-libbing for Jack. At the time, I remember thinking, "No wonder this man won eighteen majors; he had them all planned out beforehand."

After the stretching, the script continued on the range, where he gave a clinic for the eight hundred or so guests. It was clear he was excited about the course he had designed and was looking forward to playing it. As he warmed up, he gave all of us insights into his game and approach.

He started with the wedges, working on making smooth swings, before proceeding to hit short irons, mid irons, long irons, then finally the driver. He hit shots right to left, left to right, high, low. For all in attendance, there was nothing to compare with watching Jack Nicklaus up close.

As he talked, the crowd was so quiet that he probably didn't need the microphone attached to his shirt. Jack commanded respect. He looked and conducted himself like the true celebrity he is.

From the range, the group moved to the ceremony at the first tee—still right on schedule. From the tee, Jack hit a ceremonial shot with a persimmon-head, steel-shafted driver, which he later signed and gave to the club. It is displayed in the Nicklaus Gallery at the clubhouse, just outside my office.

After Jack hit a tee shot with a regular driver, one with a titanium head and graphite shaft, the spotlight shifted to me, his playing partner. I hadn't played in a month because I had been so busy trying to get the club ready for the opening, so I tried to lower my expectations. I told myself that it would just be a casual round, albeit with the greatest player ever. I knew my place this day: I was going to play fast, stay out of Jack's way, and speak only when spoken to.

Despite my attempt to deflect the pressure, I was nervous when my turn came. Sometimes, this tension can help your performance, and it certainly did so in this case. The opening hole is a par-four that stretches out to 386 yards, and the hole plays much shorter by cutting the corner of the dogleg, which is guarded by a fairway bunker. I launched a drive that flew over the sand and came to rest sixty yards past Jack's ball.

As I handed the club to my caddie, Jack caught my eye. He had a bemused look and said, somewhat playfully, "What was that all about?"

That broke the ice somewhat, and we chatted as we walked all the way down the fairway. More than eight hundred people followed us down the middle of the fairway—without gallery ropes, just like the old days.

As we walked, countless people were asking Jack for his autograph. (A member, Jude Compofelice, sensed that I was being left out and asked for mine as well.) In addition to signing autographs, Jack posed for pictures and was chatting—all at the same time.

I wasn't doing much but watching. I was caught up in the scene and found it hard to focus on playing. But Jack didn't seem to have much trouble changing gears once it was his turn to hit. The focus returned to his eyes, and he went through his famous pre-shot routine as diligently as if he were playing in a tournament. He seemed to have turned a switch.

There is a wonderful lesson here. A round of golf lasts (hopefully) four hours. That's an awfully long time to be trying to concentrate. But as Jack showed, there is no need to grind for the entire round. All you need to do is focus when it is your turn to play. Go ahead and relax and have fun between shots—after all, isn't that one of the reasons you play golf?

I don't think Jack is able to play a casual, sloppy round, and a large reason for that is that he is so disciplined when it comes to his pre-shot routine. He does the same thing time after time, as a signal to himself that it is time to focus on the shot at hand.

Another lesson you can learn from Jack is his love of winning. By this time, Jack was sixty-one. He had said good-bye to the U.S. Open and PGA Championship the previous year, and only played occasionally on the Champions and PGA Tours, at the Masters, and at his own Memorial Tournament. Jack has tremendous pride, whether in his golf game or his course designs. He loathed the idea of being a ceremonial golfer. If he didn't feel as if he had a chance to win a tournament, he simply didn't play.

With each passing year, Jack played in fewer events, which meant his fans had fewer opportunities to watch him. And he had fewer chances to demonstrate his competitive spirit.

After I had out-driven him on the first hole, we both hit our approach shots to the green. My first glimpse of his desire to outplay me came as we walked toward the putting surface. After I hit, his first comment was that his seven-iron seemed closer to the hole than my wedge. With so much else going on, he made it clear that if we were playing golf, he would be taking it seriously.

For the first several holes, we had a friendly round going. He worked out the rust in his game as he explained to the gallery the design principles of the holes. He explained the strategy for the holes, and how and why he utilized trees and bunkers. For most people, having so much in their minds would be debilitating for their games. Not for Jack.

In addition, it was clear how much passion he was bringing to the entire day. Jack had played hundreds of these opening rounds, but he seemed as excited as if this were his first. An indication of his energy level was how fast he walked from shot to shot. I had to practically jog to keep up with him.

As the round progressed, he began to elevate his game to another level. I first saw "the eye" on the sixth hole. After our approach shots, his ball was just outside mine, twenty-five feet from the hole. Jack putted first, and as he was addressing the ball, I saw a little more concentration in his face. It was a look I had seen many times before on television, coming down to the wire in major championships. Of course, he made the putt. He gave me a wink as he walked by as if to say, "Top that." It was electric being on the same course with him and feeling the concentration go up a notch.

From that point, the sense of competition between us grew. Neither of us said it, but it was clear that we were engaged in a match. But despite this underlying tension, I enjoyed every minute of watching the Golden Bear play the front nine. It was a clinic in concentration and course management.

On the ninth green, clouds started building. After we putted out, Jack's staff suggested we end the round early. I had shot even par on the front nine, and Jack was one under par.

When his people suggested to Jack that he stop playing, he responded quickly, "No way, I won't melt." It was then I knew that what had started as a friendly exhibition round had turned into a serious competition.

I don't know where my game was coming from, but I was playing well. I hit only one bad drive, on the thirteenth hole, hooking it behind a stand of trees. I was planning to chip the ball out sideways back to the fairway, but Jack walked too fast, and he and his crowd were in the way. I went to Plan B and hit a low four-iron through the trees. It was a low-percentage shot that I would never try in tournament play and one that I would never advise my students to attempt.

Somehow, the ball made it through the trees and ended up near the green. When I got to within earshot, Jack told his design team to add more trees where my ball had been—I wasn't supposed to have been able to hit that shot. I should have told Jack that I couldn't have hit that shot again with a big shag bag of balls.

By the time we reached the sixteenth hole, Jack was two shots ahead. On the green, I faced a short putt for par. Jack asked me whether I could make it.

"Yes, sir," I replied.

He motioned for me to pick it up, and off we went to the seventeenth hole.

On that green, I faced a putt of similar length to the one Jack had conceded on the previous hole. Again, he asked me if I could make it; I had the same reply.

This time, instead of conceding the putt, he said, "Prove it to me."

It was a three-footer with a little break to the right. The greens were fast and I needed to hit it firm to keep it on line. I was thrilled when the putt went in.

On the eighteenth tee, Jack was still up by two strokes. I had kept score in my head, but didn't think Jack knew where our "match" stood. I couldn't have been more wrong.

The final hole is a 567-yard par-five that I could reach in two shots and he couldn't. Jack announced to the gallery that the hole could be reached in two shots, and that he thought his opponent was going for it today. It was his way of throwing down the gauntlet, challenging me to make up the deficit that we both knew existed but had never acknowledged to each other.

I did hit two good shots and made a birdie to Jack's par. We shook hands but nothing more was said of our "match."

Jack gave a nice speech in front of the crowd on the eighteenth green and gave me some nice compliments. It's not every day Jack Nicklaus tells your new members nice things about you. And for Jack, the day was still not over. He gave a press conference, signed even more autographs, took photos seemingly with everyone who attended, and answered questions from members.

I gave Jack a ride back to the airport. Several minutes into the trip, he commented that he thought he had shot 70. Before I had a chance to reply, he quickly followed up with, "Did you have 71?"

I just smiled, having had firsthand experience against one of the most competitive golfers in history. Although his skills had slipped, his mental toughness and spirit were still very much in evidence.

MARK'S LESSONS

As a teacher, what I learned from my round with Nicklaus was more about how he handles himself and plans to play than how he swings the club. Few people talk about his swing. And few teachers hang his swing sequence on the walls of their studio for their students to examine, the way they do with Tiger Woods's or Ben Hogan's.

That Nicklaus won without a picture-perfect swing shows how prepared, disciplined, and mentally tough he was every time he teed up. And those are lessons that golfers of all abilities can benefit from—without modifying their swings.

HIGH HANDICAPPER

If you're trying to break 100, the lesson you can learn from Nicklaus is the importance of sticking to a game plan during a round. If your goal is to hit eight fairways during a round, do whatever it takes to hit those eight fairways—even if it means hitting with a five-iron off the tee. You're always in a much better position hitting from the fairway than from the rough, the trees, or in a hazard; and it will benefit you in the long run. It may be difficult to do so, but remember that Nicklaus always had a game plan and rarely deviated from it.

MID HANDICAPPER

You probably don't have a reliable shot shape yet. It can change from day to day. When you're warming up before a round, you'll find that you are hitting primarily one type of shot—draw, face, push, or pull. That will be your tendency for the day, so be disciplined about using that shot instead of fighting it, and don't try to hit shots that you cannot pull off.

For example, if you are hitting shots that go to the right and you are playing a par-three with water guarding the right side of the green, make a point to aim well left so that even a shot that goes to the right stays dry. Nicklaus was great at knowing his particular strengths and weaknesses. If you can do the same, you'll shave ample strokes off your score.

LOW HANDICAPPER

Nicklaus was the best at preparing for specific tournaments and courses. Low handicappers playing in events—club championships, member-guests—should practice the shots that they need. If you're playing a course with long par fours, practice hitting your hybrids or utility woods. Then spend plenty of time working on chips and pitches because you'll probably miss your share of greens and need to get up and down for par. Study the holes so you know when you can be aggressive and when you need to be cautious. This will allow you to make opportunistic birdies and avoid round-destroying big numbers.

ABOUT THE AUTHOR

Mark Steinbauer is an active member of The PGA of America and the
director of golf at The Club at Carlton Woods in The Woodlands, Texas. The
recipient of the 1994 Harvey Penick Teacher of the Year award and the 1996,
1999, and 2000 Horton Smith Awards, Steinbauer has taught at the Academy of Golf, the Nicklaus/Flick Golf Schools, and the Mark Steinbauer Golf
Training Center. He has made several appearances on the Golf Channel and has
contributed articles to *Golf Digest* magazine. He lives in The Woodlands, Texas,
with his wife and daughters.

ABOVE: *Mark Steinbauer (left) with his mentor Harvey Penick*

Published in 2010 by Stewart, Tabori & Chang

An imprint of ABRAMS

Library of Congress Cataloging-in-Publication Data:
Steinbauer, Mark.
  18 game-changing lessons : talking golf with legends and pros / Mark Steinbauer.
  p. cm.
  ISBN 978-1-58479-812-5
  1. Golf. 2. Golfers—Anecdotes. I. Title. II. Title: 18 game-changing lessons.
  GV965.S79 2010
  796.352—dc22   2010003755

EDITOR: Ann Stratton

DESIGNER: Glenn Gontha | gonthadesign.com

PRODUCTION MANAGER: Tina Cameron

The text of this book was composed in Mercury Display, Verlag, and Poplar.

Printed and bound in the United States of America

10 9 8 7 6 5 4 3 2 1

Stewart, Tabori & Chang books are available at special discounts when purchased in quantity for premiums and promotions as well as fundraising or educational use. Special editions can also be created to specification. For details, contact specialsales@abramsbooks.com or the address below.

ABRAMS
THE ART OF BOOKS SINCE 1949

115 West 18th Street
New York, NY 10011
www.abramsbooks.com

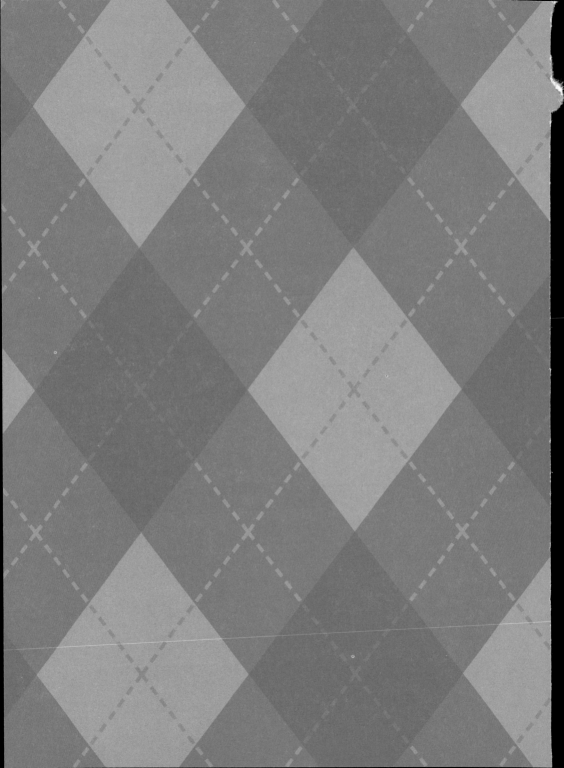